Hocking, William
Ernest

The meaning of
immortality in
human experience

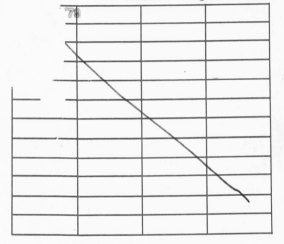

THE MEANING OF IMMORTALITY
IN HUMAN EXPERIENCE

The Ingersoll Lecture on
the Immortality of Man
Harvard University, 1936
MEANINGS OF DEATH

The Hiram W. Thomas Lecture
University of Chicago, 1936
MEANINGS OF LIFE

The Agnes A. and Constantine E. A. Foerster
Lecture on the Immortality of the Soul
University of California, Berkeley, 1942
THE RELATIVITY OF DEATH

WILLIAM ERNEST HOCKING

THE MEANING
OF IMMORTALITY
IN
HUMAN EXPERIENCE

Including

THOUGHTS ON DEATH AND LIFE

Revised

GREENWOOD PRESS, PUBLISHERS
WESTPORT, CONNECTICUT

Library of Congress Cataloging in Publication Data

Hocking, William Ernest, 1873-1966.
    The meaning of immortality in human experience,
including Thoughts on death and life.

    Published in 1937 under title: Thoughts on death and
life.
    1. Death. 2. Life. 3. Immortality (Philosophy)
I. Title.
[BD421.H62 1973]   128'.5   72-10697
ISBN 0-8371-6621-7

Originally published in 1957 by Harper & Brothers Publishers,
New York

Reprinted with the permission of Harper & Row, Publishers, Inc.

First Greenwood Reprinting 1973
Second Greenwood Reprinting 1975

Library of Congress Catalog Card Number 72-10697

ISBN 0-8371-6621-7

Printed in the United States of America

To

ARCHIBALD ALLAN BOWMAN

*Strong, fervent, knightly spirit
who saw the vastness
of common things*

CONTENTS

PREFACE TO
THE REVISED AND
ENLARGED EDITION

THE title of this book has intentional reference to the title of my first book, *The Meaning of God in Human Experience*, published some half-century ago. Like that earlier book, it intends to assert that present human experience has something to say about matters commonly regarded as out of the range of empirical knowledge. Most careful thinkers today, those who agree with Kant and those who disagree with him about the limits of human knowledge, are inclined to accept his judgment that God, Freedom, and Immortality, as metaphysical notions, have no scientific standing; and that any credence we give them must be in the nature of an act of faith or of a postulate based on our moral convictions. If "experience" is to be identified in its scope with the reach of our senses plus the thoughtful interpretation of sense-data, Kant's judgment must stand.

I deny that experience is thus limited.

In that earlier book I made a radical assertion which I am now reasserting and applying to the idea of immortality:

> I venture to say that unless God does operate within experience in an identifiable manner, speculation will not find him,

and may be abandoned. The need for metaphysical thought
arises (I venture the paradox) *just because* God is a matter
of experience, because he works there and is known there in
his works. [Page 216]

The task of metaphysics is not to fly away from experience into the inaccessible; it is to interpret the data
of experience in their full range, depth, and wonder, including the data of sense. The first principle of our work
is that in experience we are inescapably dealing, not with
"phenomena" alone, but with reality: no single human
action can allow that its *pou sto* is pure "appearance."
Recognize this, and at once "empiricism" takes on a
higher dignity. We recover for philosophic thought a
pertinence to the daily concerns of mankind, and bring
the topics of God and Immortality into tangible significance for the actual struggles and passions, also the intuitions, of the human lot.

On the face of it, it seems less pertinent to speak of
immortality as having meaning in human experience than
to speak thus of God. When Charles Lindbergh says "I
now realize that [God's] presence can be sensed in every
sight and act and incident" (*Of Flight and Life*, p. 52),
he is speaking of experience, not of speculation: he speaks
as a practical man, concerned with the most tangible of
issues, the survival of our civilization. But immortality
is in a different case: is not immortality by definition just
beyond the scope of experience? In what sense can it have
a present meaning? Does my title not run the risk of
offering a contradiction in terms?

Let me make clear what I mean by the terms of the
title.

It will generally be granted that *the Idea* of immortality has a present significance. I mean this; but I also mean much more.

As for the Idea, it does indeed directly affect the time-field of all conscious life; for all human action proceeds on the basis of some notion of the time-perspective toward the future. The early decades of human life look forward into a non-terminating future—I do not say an affirmatively infinite future, but a future simply *not closed* (as the etymology of the word in-finite fairly suggests). In this formally negative, but potentially fertile, sense, our natural human time-vista contains *all the future*. And while the particular event-contents of that endless reach vanish swiftly into shadow, we do not leave it a pure vacuum: we accept the kindly aid of our technical astrophysics, as far as its physical probabilities will carry; and as for the fortunes of the conscious-and-personal denizens of the cosmos, no concern of astro-physics—they remain themes for prophecy and imagination. Since time empty of events is time no longer; and since time cannot check its own forward reach; each one of us willy nilly must have images of some sort for its filling. And whether those images be definite, or poetic, or dubious blur, or flitting subjective shadows evoked by cautious refusal-to-explore the cavern, that future-field as a whole casts its temper even now on the felt significance of one's life and of every deed issuing from it. Though the vista is post-mortem, the significance is not post-mortem, but present and pervasive.

Most post-Kantian discussions of immortality have been concerned in this way with the influence of *the Idea*, whether as postulate or as faith. And we shall be concerned with this meaning. But my further proposal is that *unless an Idea has or can have an intelligible basis in the constitution of things* it is illegitimate, whether for postulate or for faith: we must be able to say what it is we postulate or believe. With this proposal, I assume responsibility for an inquiry into the actual conditions under which alone the Idea of immortality could be legitimate.

The responsibility is heavy. But without such inquiry we face the momentum of scientific advance with simply a reluctant protest. The strong presumption against any survival of death has its grounds in the natural conditions of all human life, conditions increasingly well understood. We are organisms, highly complex. We cannot claim, nor could we wish, the sort of perpetuity proper to protozoa and other unicellular organisms. We grow, and we age, body and mind alike. Senescence, the "growing-old" which is a sort of un-growing, and which Weismann considered a property inherent in all metazoa, appeared to him not only universal in this group but also beneficial, since "unlimited duration of life of the individual would be a senseless luxury." [1] The naturalism of today and every day which accepts Nature as its final source of instruction can speak with no other voice. And men like old Lucretius or newer Bertrand Russell or Corliss Lamont, who draw their literal conclusions without flinching, deserve our respect for their clear speaking. The science for which they speak is not an alien voice; it is *our* science, yours and mine. It must be in full view of its cumulative force that any one today examines the conditions in our present human constitution and its "environment" (otherwise known as "reality") which entail a possibility of the personal survival of death. If there are any such condi-

[1] A. Weismann, *Ueber die Dauer des Lebens,* Jena, 1882. Quoted by A. Comfort, *The Biology of Senescence,* 1956, p. 9.

tions even now present in the human self, they will show themselves in human experience: immortality, not as idea alone but as potential of structure, will have a present meaning there. This is the second and definitive aspect of our title.

*   *   *

This book is not a systematic treatise planned as a whole in advance. It has grown. Its main ingredients represent responses to occasions calling on me to summarize my views on human destiny as they then stood. Three such occasions are here involved, and their results are recorded with substantial faithfulness in the text, with respect to the identity of the occasion, even though the responses on my part may show varying stages of insight.

These were: the Ingersoll Lecture on Immortality, at Harvard, entitled "Meanings of Death" (1936) ; the Hiram W. Thomas Lecture, at the University of Chicago (later in 1936), entitled "Meanings of Life"; the Foerster Lecture on Immortality, at the University of California, Berkeley, entitled "The Relativity of Death" (1942). The two earlier lectures were published together in 1937, as *Thoughts on Death and Life,* with certain minor changes and additions in the interest of a consecutive argument. The Foerster Lecture, though I had hoped to publish it sooner, only now appears, in its main argument, as the fifth and final Part of this book, preceded by an Interlude taking note of certain changes in the temper of thought during the twenty-year interval.

The earlier occasions were concerned chiefly with the question whether the continuance of life after death is *desirable* in the sense that it is something which in a universe based on a moral order *ought to be*. The further and substantive question whether such survival is *possible* was barely opened. In the last few pages of the Ingersoll Lecture, I sketched the issues and certain lines of a conceivable answer; but I was not then ready to embark on the thoroughgoing metaphysical analysis called for.

When, some five years later, the third occasion arose, I was more nearly prepared to offer the needed analysis. That readiness had arrived in a curiously dated way, making its own occasion. The story, immaterial in itself, may offer some illustration of the special point on which understanding seemed to turn.

I had been engaged during the Fall of 1941 in a seminar on metaphysics at Harvard. We had been discussing newer views of space and time, mass and energy. Metaphysical speculation and physical theory had become inseparable; but both, at this moment of world history, appeared remote from the pressing anxieties of men: Europe was deep in war; we were verging toward involvement. Yet somehow, relativity-theory seemed to carry us toward the center of things, since the unlocking of physical riddles must affect all human doings, including war itself. After a meeting of the seminar, late Wednesday afternoon, October 21, I went for a lonely walk along Charles River bank.

> The sun had already set. A new crescent was standing over the far end of Andersen bridge. The mass of Business School buildings was reflected in the river as a dimly waving blackness. Under the blackness the river was silver. Against the silver, a Harvard eight at belated practice, was silhouetted, oarsmen and coxwain posturing rhythmically like gondoliers.
>
> To the west, over the line of gray-blue hills, a rim of brownish-red glow, shading upward into a sky-depth of lumi-

nous darkness. It was as though for the moment Nature were holding still—caught in a spell of quiet and tense glory, unwilling to fade.

Illusion or not, the beauty and infinite quietude of a scene, whose inner texture was doubtless infinite motion, invaded the witness, as if its repose were the truth. Here was quiescence —no seminar, no discussion, no labor of categories, also no war. Time had stopped, and the world was now drenched in unmoving space. Space was endless; it was *my* space, running out far beyond the solitary evening star; running also through the earth, and out the other side. There were armies at night, minds full of battle-plans for tomorrow's action. Was it truly the same space? Could that space, crowded with fighters' strategies, be the same as my space, spell-bound in peace?

Yes, it must be the identical space; it is the same world for all of us. Yet it cannot be the same. For no one else saw the world I saw; if I had not happened along, that marvel of a sky-moment might have passed unknown. It was certainly not known *to itself*, was it? Those colors, lights, shadows, shapes, could exist only for a creature with eyes, stationed at or near where I was standing.

Our various spaces, all infinite, must be and cannot be identical. The answer? *Space is not single, but plural.* There is a world-space, identical for all included persons. But for each one, there is also a private space, perhaps spaces, holding private responses to qualities, holding also futurities, not yet existent—plans, battle-plans perhaps, plans that can be detained, modified, canceled, as events in the identical world-space cannot be.

Space must have a plural—this we were saying in the seminar. And more than this, each person envisages plural spaces. Then, the *position of the person,* the self, toward this his plurality, how shall we describe it? Each space can be called a "field," a continuum in which infinite positions, potentials, etc., can be distinguished and held-together. Could the self, as envisaging plural fields, be *a field of fields?*

The walk away from the seminar had brought me back to the seminar; or no: it had brought the seminar back to me, but in a vivid picture-presence. What I there thought, I was here *seeing*. It was all simple and self-evident; but I had a feeling of admission, as if a difficulty had dropped away. That night a brief article went off to the Journal, introduced as follows:

> A relatively unilluminating compactness has some compensating advantages, the chief of which is, in a time of war, that one can get it said.[2]

The enduring perception contained in this very momentary experience is that of the self as a field of fields. This expression is open to technical criticism both from the side of psychology and from that of field-theory—the analogy is imperfect. But as it is used in this book, it is valid. It opens the way to a doctrine of concrete freedom, and to a view of the conditions of possible survival of death, which I trust may serve as an aid in the age-long inquiry into the tenable meaning of immortality. It should offer grounds for distinguishing what is purely imaginative and poetic in the other-worldly gropings of mankind from what is, on the one hand, ultimate mystery, and on the other, empirical truth.

WILLIAM ERNEST HOCKING

Madison, New Hampshire
June 22, 1957

---

[2] The paper was published in *Journal of Philosophy*, December 4, 1941. I had added a few words to the last sentence, making it, "One can get it said, perhaps even read!", an addition which the event showed over-sanguine. December 7, Pearl Harbor.

PREFACE TO
THOUGHTS ON DEATH
AND LIFE

THESE brief meditations on great themes make no pretense to be adequate. They are serious in intent and, I believe, pertinent to the present stage of thinking about the meaning of human life and its destiny. But it will not require an experienced eye to see signs of unfinishedness. They retain much of the character of the conversations and of the two lectures out of which they arose—the Ingersoll Lecture given at Harvard University on April 21, 1936, and the Thomas Lecture given at the University of Chicago on May 14, 1936. For the sake of clarity I have expanded the text somewhat beyond that of the lectures as delivered. I have not attempted to avoid a few repetitions: they too may add something to clarity and will at least register the truth that the meaning of life and the meaning of death are inseparable.

If the brevity of the book requires justification it is in substance the same as that of the spoken words on which it is based. They were addressed to actual questions: and an actual question may remain as effectively unanswered if it is replied to at theoretically ample length as if the response is delayed until it can be perfect. If one is asked abruptly, "What do you now think about death? or of the immortality of man? or of the total sense of human life?", assuredly one's first impulse is silence; nevertheless, there may be that in the temper or need out of which the demand comes to cancel that impulse and require an offering of the state of one's reasonings at the moment. One need not profess finality; he must acknowledge the darkness which borders the edge of his exploring range, and also invades it. But there exist current errors which can be rectified. And there are dogmatic, seeming-scientific negations which are at least as footless as dogmatic affirmations and whose vulnerability it may be at this moment even more imperative to expose.

There are no concerns which more pervasively affect human happiness and sanity, both at the conscious and at the subconscious level, than these issues with which we are here dealing: my aim is to remove some of the needless obstacles to a just judgment.

WILLIAM ERNEST HOCKING

Cambridge, Massachusetts
January 7, 1937

PART I

MEANINGS OF DEATH

PROLOGUE

THE problem of the survival of death by human persons is an empirical problem for which we have no empirical evidence. It is a question of fact, and of fact in time, for which there are no antecedent probabilities one way or the other. Human survival is neither probable nor improbable, because we have to approach it through those same questions of world order which include the basis of probability.

As a philosophical problem, it is a secondary chapter, a corollary of other views, such as the structure of the world, the existence of a God interested in persons, freedom, the relation of mind and body. It is a last chapter, or perhaps an appendix, of the usual system of metaphysics.

Hence it is a theme in which many people have lost interest because they have taken their answer, Yes or No, with their general world view. It is settled in the affirmative or (more frequently today) in the negative by what they otherwise believe; it is no longer a question—and if it were, not a separate question.

The function of this discussion is not to prove immortality, nor to disprove it. It is to shake ourselves out of sophistication about it, to disturb customary attitudes in an effort to see afresh the nature of the question, to estimate its importance or unimportance, to get once more its original impact on the mind of the self-conscious creature, in the hope of arriving at a clearer total perception of what is significant and what is possible.

I propose that we approach the problem from the obverse side, by way of the meanings of death.

I

INCREDULITY TOWARD DEATH

Man is the only animal that contemplates death, and also the only animal that shows any sign of doubt of its finality. This does not mean that he doubts it as a future fact. He accepts his own death, with that of others, as inevitable, plans for it, provides for the time when he shall be out of the picture. Yet, not less today than formerly, he confronts this fact with a certain incredulity regarding the scope of its destruction.

This incredulity is due partly but not wholly to his wishes. It is first of all a phase of the general suspicion with which all obvious judgments about human destiny come to be regarded: the philosopher who offers the plain and primary facts presented in sensation and perception as also the final facts seem to the plain man the truly credulous person.

And in the special article of death, he has from his own self-consciousness an item which proves nothing, but which intimates a possibility. As a witness of death, now and then the death of a friend, he finds in himself a double response, not a single one: he is defeated in the most signal manner by the physical forces out of which human life emerges— he appreciates this defeat; and it is just then, when the evidence is most complete, that he experiences a vague and hesitant resurgence of confidence. It is as if that defeat were the experience necessary to remind him of something in himself which his everyday self-awareness overlooks, something which at one point breaks through the closed frame of "nature," holds its own in independence of what happens within "nature," and which might conceivably jut out immune beyond the catastrophe of death. In this contradictory eddy of emotion which psychologists well understand—if analogies constitute understanding—the scientific conscience is prone to see perversity. The common man, however, protests that he is not being led by his emotion; that his emotion is rather a result than a cause; that he has been admitted to a momentary glimpse of objective fact in the structure of things; and that it is this fact which justifies him in ascribing to his wishes in this region a modest evidential value.

So far as wish enters into the situation, it is clear that the wish is not primarily for himself. It takes the form of a demand that someone else, whose death has been witnessed, shall not have perished from the universe. Attachments have been broken off, the emotional habits of life have been thwarted, but the protest is not leveled against this personal pain. It is leveled against the destruction of something admirable. It has little or nothing in common with the demand found by Kant in human conscience, calling for endless time in which this moral self may become perfect! On the contrary, it is a cry that life *has produced* the perfect being, beloved by me, and has thrown it away. I care enough for that appearance to carve it into imperishable stone, yet nature lets the living original perish! It is a protest which moves far beyond personal suffering and expresses outrage at an objective unfitness.

Thus the notion of survival arises far more as a claim of right than as a personal wish. It is based less on the law of individual duty than on the right of affection and an aesthetic justice. It is conceived as the obligation of the universe to us before it is our duty to the universe.

The interest in survival has another noteworthy peculiarity. Most desires are desires for specific objects. This desire is not for an object, but for a subject. It contemplates in the first instance, not the satisfaction of any wish, but the continuance of wishing and of the wisher.

In this respect it is like the will to live, which has no definite object of pursuit, but merely drives toward the maintenance of the consciousness of objects-in-general, and is therefore sometimes put down by psychologists as a piece of mythology. But the fact is there: the extraordinary concern which men commonly show in mere being-alive, regardless of whether the actual contents of experience are pleasant or unpleasant. Surgeons now recognize that beside the dread of pain, which anaesthesia was invoked to allay, and the further dread of the knife, which anaesthesia can partially displace, there is a distinct dread of anaesthesia itself, a dread of being put out of the reach of one's aliveness, which in some persons is strong enough to lead them to prefer the undimmed pain of an operation. It is a paradoxical interest in consciousness itself as distinct from the contents of consciousness—a distinction which has its own scientific value.

Is this empty interest irrational? It may seem a vestige of unintelligent animal tenacity-of-life; yet we reflect that unless there are subjects and knowers in the world, there are either no values at all, or else no takers for such values as might be conceived to exist. We might imagine, as among the possible worlds, one particularly hard world in which every particular human wish up to the present moment has been disappointed; yet that world, taken in its entire sweep, need be neither hopeless nor meaningless. But a world devoid of conscious subjects is necessarily a meaningless world. An interest in the survival of conscious subjects, merely in their capacity as necessary conditions for conserving the meaning of things, may well be an instinctive sign of a deeper rationality.

So far, I am concerned merely to point out some of the motives of the belief in survival of death, and to clear our minds of the prevalent but absurd notion that it is based on wishes alone or on wishes essentially selfish.

But we ought also to note that incredulity toward death is only partial; and that notions of survival, reinforced by crowd consciousness and enshrined in the bold assertions of religion, are in most persons only half-sure of themselves, and therefore subject to an alternate Yes and No.

The early men who first conceived survival lost the courage of their affections, and dampened down their idea of the surviving spirit into the melancholy picture of a ghost. And later men, conspiring to preserve intact the perishing memories of the dead, substituted for the flickering medium of remembrance the assumed stabilities of wood, stone, bronze. The physical monument appeared a safer basis of endurance than the mental fact upon its own ground. It is no small part of the pathos of the mortuary customs of all religions—this mute element of doubt which infects the heart of faith, and makes the Christian cemetery a vast invocation of matter to support the hesitant certainties of the immaterial.

The natural attitude toward death remains thus double and antithetical. At one moment we say, Death is an appearance and not an end. At the next, Death is real and final, it is fantastic to think otherwise. No doctrine of survival in any case escapes the universal fact of death, nor the suffering that goes with it: these remain the data of every argument.

POSITIVE MEANINGS OF DEATH

IF there is to be any chance of seeing beyond death, we must first be able to see death as it is. And to see death truly, we must recognize what meaning it has both for the race and for the individual who dies.

It is customary to look upon death as unmixed evil, perhaps the severest of evils. Pessimists have taken it as their crowning argument, forgetting that if life is an evil, death which is only the expunging of life must be a good. But if life is a good, as for common consciousness it is, and if in death the self comes to nothing and remains forever nothing for itself, then death must be the major calamity. And if the final state of things gives us the lasting sum of their values, we can hardly avoid the reflection of Tolstoi, that an ultimate annihilation sends its shadow backward and cancels the worth of every present achievement. Religion reflects the universal feeling of the evil of death when it calls it the wages of sin.

But if death is the price of anything, biological death, it is the price not of sin but of love. For if men by way of love are to beget new generations of men continually, the old must pass. The world room is finite; without perennial death there could be no perennial appearance of childhood. Without childhood, love which is transmission, and whose greatest joy is the handing-on of life, would be choked in its beginnings. Love is the distant acceptance and celebration of one's own transiency. And death, when it comes, should be the glad remembrance and celebration of love.

For the race, death means flexibility in the changes of history. Death renders it unnecessary to be forever educating old men to new ways; for as the old men pass, their rigid formulae pass with them. A suit of armor cast in long pieces—even flexible pieces—is an enemy to agility; but made of tiny flakes or links—even if each one is inflexible—it lends itself to all the supple bendings of the body. Were Adam, Noah, Socrates, Confucius still among us, how we would weary of the daily rumor of their views upon the affairs of the moment: would not a certain sense of fair play bring about a conspiracy to ignore them, so that contemporary voices might sound out with due sonority and weight? If there were no natural death, society might well be driven to institute some form of artificial death, such as an honorable ostracism, lest the cumulative weight of great authority hold all new-arriving tongues locked in deference and thwart their arrival at maturity through the exercise of responsible opinion.

It is not merely that the old become static—that need not be the case—but they frequently become wise and prudent. And life must progress in part by the imprudence of those who undertake the impossible, not knowing what they do. It is death which insures that the reins shall leave sagacious and experienced hands and come to the unwisdom of youth, with the large probability of new ills but also of a modicum of good otherwise unattainable.

Without death, the inequalities of age alone would become monstrous, and the growing emotional disparity between ancients and beginners insupportable. And so far as there operates in society the rule that to him that hath shall be given, all the geometrically-growing advantages of power and prestige require a natural terminus if they are not to destroy the access of man to man on which society rests. They find this terminus in the democracy of death: a rude mechanical justice, operating without noise, incessantly reduces to common dust all the mounting conquests of personal prowess and distributes their yield to new hands. And if men incline to the opinion that such and such great figure is indispensable, death furnishes the experimental proof that no man is necessary to the race, and so the sanity of the species, always running to the ease and vicarious elevations of hero worship, is from time to time restored.

Further, the fact that life has a time limit allows it to have shape and character. Its work can·be summed and considered as a whole: it stands for an identifiable something.

Retain Plato in life for two thousand years, growing and producing great works as a Plato must until he parallels the entire history of Western thought—for what, then, in our minds could Plato stand, and who could think or write about Plato? Biography is baffled unless a life, limited like a work of art, becomes in some sense the song of its own time, having indeed an epoch of its own, and a limited output into the public treasury. It is with the death of an artist that his work first begins to find its valuation and its historic emplacement.

The vessel which contains a life remains plastic and unfinished, until death—having its whole contents—rounds-in its end; then one can speak of the quality of that life and of the shape of that vessel; and these become the meaning to the world of that personal name. Perhaps we may say that the thing we call "individuality" is not a pre-existing fact but rather a possibility until death finishes the definition. Then alone is this person a complete qualitative fact, distinct from every other.

These considerations among many give death a positive value to the world at large as it witnesses the coming and going of its members. Humanity as a procession is better than humanity as a fixture; and flux, even in the sphere of values, appears to have superiority over the ancient category of substance.

But to the individual who dies, or who is to die—what can death mean to him? It is a matter of course that each individual imbibes the general view of death current in his society: if this current view is resigned to his passing, it becomes him as a man to assume the same attitude; and most men successfully do so, partly because the general view comes to them first and with the vastest possible authority, since all but himself can think of his death as the death of an *other*. But to the dier, his own death is a lonely experience which society, unable to enter, is to this extent disqualified to judge. The partial philosophic reconciliation of the social mind to his own disappearance must, while it alleviates, contribute also an added pang, and emphasize the solitude of the event.

We must note that the belief in one's own death is an

acquired and usually a late belief, not at all a native one. The immediate feeling of life touches no limit either of beginning or end: to be alive is to expect that each next moment will be followed by another. Consciousness is not a targeted attention to instantly present data alone; it is also a reaching forward and backward in time, relating what is to what was and to what is coming. And the logic of this character of consciousness is apparent: since it can only exist as time-spinning in this way, a moment which had no next moment would not be a conscious moment. Hence a last moment of consciousness (as well as a first moment) is logically impossible. Neither terminus of life can be experienced; and neither can be realized in imagination. Hence the belief which every mature man acquires that his own death will come, is an intellectual adoption, not an intuitive faith.

This situation explains something of that incredulity which we first remarked, and which continues to attend one's thought of his own death, even if it is banished from the general thought of human destiny. But the common mortality of man must eventually come home to every Socrates. And with the first shock of the deduction, which has the force of a painful discovery, that I, too, shall die, there comes a stern practical consequence—a tendency to curb my farther-reaching purposes and to deal anxiously with time as with an infinitely precious because absolutely limited quantity.

Here one finds the first positive value of his own death. For it is only through this reflection that one realizes the nature of time.

To have endless time to squander on each task leaves one a stranger to the instancy of the moment—its once-onlyness, its *Einmaligkeit*! To perceive that the number of available "nows" is finite and that no "now" recurs is to know what temporal quality is, irreversible, undetainable, inexorable. The "present" assumes an office—it becomes recognized as the invisible portal through which Destiny enters, and silently, under my hands, takes on unalterable shapes. I begin to consider a certain time span as the locus of my life: I become identified with that era; it is in one sense, a quantum which I own. The future is always the region of possibility; but now that a boundary is drawn at its outer limit, it has the added character of "opportunity," an opportunity which is single and unique. Of this self, there will be no more and no other than what this finite time shall in fact contain. Now for the first time I truly *enter into time*; and this sober arrival, the true date of my human maturity, is a stage of being which, once experienced, I could not willingly forgo.

For human maturity, bringing with it the pervasive reconstruction of all purposes, by the recognition of *limit*, is a notable advance in self-knowledge. Still, such acceptance of death is hardly the same as a reconciliation with death. One continues to think and hope impossible things about prolonging life, or of transposing its unfinished activities to another sphere. But in due time one perceives another aspect of the situation—namely, that living tends to produce the mental conditions for its own closing.

We hear of the biological life cycle, the maturing and the running-down of the body, the accompanying loss of mental savor and enterprise. We take it for granted that in this decline it is the physical failure which slowly inflicts itself upon the mind, so that death actually begins long before it is consummated, solely because the body has passed its zenith. Why does it not occur to us that there is also a mental life cycle whereby, even without the aid of the body, a welcome is prepared for death?

Consider this: that living, for a human being, is a series of decisions; and that each decision has the effect of rendering actual what was previously a mere possibility, one among many. Before I decide, my field of possibility has a certain generality and freedom; when I have acted, one possibility is, as we say, "realized," the others are abandoned and thus in effect destroyed. And this one which is realized is pinned down, dated, and entangled with all the circumstances of its particular time and place. So long as I merely wish to eat, I remain free as to what I eat and where; but if I am to continue in existence I must abandon this freedom and come to the actual decision to eat: I must settle on a place and an hour and commit myself to the food then and there available and all its associations. My best foresight is incomplete, so that in choosing I perforce accept much that I have not chosen. In brief, decision must traffic with the facts at hand, and in so doing take *their* color, *their* manner, *their* moment: decision descends into a world of irrelevant particulars, is compromised with a measure of irrationality, and without this cannot touch the ground of concrete existence.

There are persons who keenly feel and resent this stain involved in decision, this acceptance of arbitrary datedness in one's purpose, this descent into irrationality. They are pained by the necessity of decision, scrutinize all their attachments, defer commitment, remain aloof from party-belonging, from institutions, even from friendships, since "friends must descend to meet." But to remain aloof is to die before one begins to live. There is no choice but to immerse oneself in the stream of history, accept one's time location, breathe-in the contaminations of tradition, become defined as the man of this issue, this party, this emergency.

The mind is at home with its ideas, especially with the ideal possibilities it has built out of the material of imagination; as imaginative, they are "figments"; but as containing the ingredients of value, they claim loyalty as well as desire. But living is a continuous marriage of idea with fact, and like every bridal, on one hand it fulfills one's destiny and on the other limits one's infinitude. Hence it is that mingling with all one's attachments there arises a factor of detachment, a growing tide of criticism of those accidental and irrelevant traits which, accepted with each decision, accumulate as a sediment in self-consciousness. And with this, as the passage of time renders it sensible of its own purport, there arises an impulse to revert to the original wholeness and freedom. One stands less and less under the spell of the excited emphases, the eloquent self-proclaimed importances of the current world, or one adopts the illusion of momentousness in the passing show with a touch of will, as an habitué of the drama. New enterprises attract but fall short of conviction; familiar sayings stir familiar feelings but without dominating the will; a broadening sympathy dilutes the energies of efficiency: the scale of one's values takes its proportion increasingly from moods of serenity, less and less from the enthusiasms and pugnacities of the arena. And death thereby acquires yet a new meaning.

For death begins to mean freedom from the acquired load and burden of the irrational. *This* self, scarred, marked, identified, dated, need not live forever. Coming as a release and as forgiveness for the untruth of the pragmatic personality, death appears with a fitness, a necessity, even a beauty of its own. In this way, living generates in the mind, as well as in the body, a certain willingness to die.

In point of fact, these tempers characteristic of natural age are to some extent always present. For the capacity to regard my particular life as a special object of thought, and so as something separate from the self that judges it—something to be prized but also estimated, criticized and for due cause renounced—this is the special mark of humanity.

I am not altogether free in any action (young or old) so long as I am dominated by an inescapable will to live. Under the spell of that instinct, life appears precious above all things, and no good however great could justify its sacrifice: for when consciousness is gone, there is nothing. As I think of it, I become obsessed by the necessity of living, which means holding to the life I have with a desperate tenacity: and the ordinary risks which men take gladly—the risks of soldier, miner, aviator, traveler, nay, of the common deeds of eating, conversing, losing one's guard in sleep, become forms of madness.

As contrasted with such rational—and craven—fascination with living, the willingness to die appears as a necessary condition of normal life, and a well-considered acceptance of death as a new stage of freedom. The power of suicide—whether the act itself be base or noble, whether it be direct, or the indirect suicide of a Socrates or a Jesus, of men who live too dangerously for natural death—is an exalted power. Property is not mine until I can alienate it: life is not mine until I can renounce it.

This type of freedom is peculiarly marked in our own day; and though it disguises itself under the mask of an ironic humor which refuses to take too seriously the only thing of serious import to oneself, it is one sign of the inner greatness of this age. It has been a condition without which the best advances of our science, medicine, technology could hardly have occurred. Tagore, in rebuking the notion that the civilization of the West is "materialistic" as compared with the "spiritual" quality of the Orient, has well recorded this quality underlying our technological advance:

> When the aeroplane rises into the sky, we may marvel at it as the acme of mechanical perfection. But it is more than this: it is a victory of the spirit. For it was not until, in the West, man had overcome the fear of death that he could master the art of flying—the art of the gods!

Through death, then, life becomes a surveyable object, distinct from myself, which I can on occasion and with good will put away. And this may be the beginning of seeing beyond death. But whether this is truth or fancy cannot be judged until we attend to the logical analysis which underlies our ideas of life and death.

III

LOGICAL PRELIMINARIES

UNNECESSARY IMPEDIMENTS

THERE is an aroma of triviality attending most argument about immortality. One seems to be considering a competition between a disruptive force, death, and a cohesive force, personal consciousness, somewhat on the analogy of the competition between the penetrative power of projectiles and the resistance of armor plate, as if a victory in favor of survival could be scored by showing that the soul has a certain tensile strength. Or as if it were a question of the articles of association between mind and body, whether a partnership or an identity. If the two are identical, the death of the body is the death of the mind; if the two are simply associates, then death may mean the dissolution of a partnership, in which the mind is set free from an intimate bond, and may conceivably move on alone, or spin another relationship.

Instinctive distaste for such argumentation is a symptom that the grounds of decision on this issue are not to be found in the play of concepts, but belong rather to that region in which the felt values of things legislate for our sense of truth. Nevertheless, we are not justified in the evasion of logical issues; for it is the particular function of logic to bring consistency into our views, trivial or important, and to clear away unnecessary confusions. It is seldom that the careful definition of a problem fails to bring to light something of its answer.

There is a brand of logic which would exclude in advance all occupation with this problem on the ground that it is speculative and therefore meaningless. This critique, promising a vast economy of thought, is in accord with the positivist temper which professes to extract all its meanings from hard facts, the modern method of milking stones. But the logic of the positivist here falls into fallacy. For, as we pointed out at the beginning, the problem of survival is not speculative in its immediate nature: it is a question of empirical fact; it is concerned with events in time. A "survival" which should imply a passage out of time into timelessness would not indeed be devoid of meaning: in a minor degree it is a common experience (as in absent-mindedness), and in its ideal perfection, it is for Vedantists like Vivekananda the final stage of the soul's journey. But this is not what we (or they) mean by survival. In case of one's own survival, it is an issue of future fact. In the case of the survival of persons already dead, it is an issue of present fact: are they or are they not now living and aware of anything?

To say that it is an empirical question is to say that its answer may be verified in experience. But this is the peculiarity of the question: that it cannot be verified by us, but only by the survivors. If there are survivors, death is most obviously the cessation of our ordinary communication with them. I do not raise the question of parapsychological experience; I appeal here simply to the common situation in which we accept doors as closed, and empirical evidence of their survival as inaccessible.

It is for this reason that we are driven to approach the problem indirectly, through speculative channels. But the absence of direct verifiability no more justifies us in banishing the question than the absence of intercourse between Peru and Spain in A.D. 1400 could have justified a denial by either of the existence of the other.

The problem of immortality, then, is a nonspeculative question which depends for its answer on speculative questions; and these speculative questions, because something particular depends on them, are saved from being meaningless, by the most positive of positivistic criteria.

It is this necessary reference to the wider world view which takes the problem out of the region of probability or improbability, where for most contemporary appraisal it seems to lie. It is, for example, a common judgment that in view of the close association of mind and brain, survival is improbable. This is to speak loosely. If there is a strict co-variation between brain action and mental action, survival is not improbable but impossible. The element of doubt attaches not to the inference but to the reasoning which sets up the premise, the alleged co-variation. If that premiss is in error, the exclusion of survival fails, and fails not by gradual steps, but completely. There are no intermediate degrees of probability.

This illustrates our thesis that survival is neither probable nor improbable, in advance of a determination of one's world view or metaphysics. For metaphysics undertakes to determine what sorts of order and disorder exist in the world; and it is on the ground of these types of order that the probability of any sort has to be judged. A

given type of order may exclude survival; another type
of order may require it; a third type of order may show
survival to be possible under certain conditions. In no
case are we dealing with probabilities.

This analysis might lead us to expect that something
like a proof might be forthcoming, either that survival
takes place, or that it is impossible. And some men do in
fact attain conviction, by way of their general view of
the world. If they believe that the universe has a unity
and a dominating purpose, or makes on the whole some
sort of sense, they are prone to conclude that the minds
of men must be able somehow to carry on their adventure.
If they adopt the view that human life and consciousness
are episodes in a world which as a whole has no purposive
structure, but is in its last analysis plain physical fact,
they are bound to consider survival both meaningless and
impossible.

But as a matter of human history, those who affirm immortality have usually been more hopeful than certain,
whereas those who deny it have commonly regarded their
position as having the force of a demonstration. I am per-
sonally little impressed by the proofs which have been
offered for the immortality of the soul. That the soul is
intrinsically indestructible, because of its absolute simplicity or its character as a substance, I do not believe.
The distinction above referred to, between an identity of
mind and body and an association of mind with body,
seems to me of logical value, but of no great force in this
problem; for the alliance of mind and body is in any case
so close that we cannot regard either as a complete entity
without the other, nor acquit the mind of responsibility
for what its body does.

Nor am I convinced by the usual idealistic arguments, derived from the prior reality of the subject self with reference to its objects. It is true that the human knower collaborates in building up its world of objects, for knowing is interpreting, and interpreting is acting. But the human self is not the sole author of its objects, nor does it construct at its own free choice: its production must be a reproduction or it is false. The ego is thus dependent on outer reality, even while it acts; and if it were severed from the original sources of its own object world, the remaining self would hardly be a complete person, nor capable of life.

I find more satisfaction in an involuntary argument which might be drawn from a diametrically opposite world view, whether in the form of materialism, or naturalism, or realism, or technical behaviorism. This type of view, which approaches all understanding of mental facts from the side of the nervous system, and excludes on principle every appeal to consciousness as a factor in the activity of the organism, has to regard the mind as a fact for which it has no use, and for which therefore it can offer no explanation. For the behaviorist the operating organism would be a much neater affair, and would act just the same, if it were not conscious. He cannot, of course, deny the existence of the fact of consciousness, at least in his own person; and he assumes that the human bodies around him are attended by this same useless phenomenon. He therefore talks with us, his fellow men, and feels sorry for us when we seem to be ailing. But the presence of consciousness in the world puzzles him. It ought not to be there, on his premises. And the inference he ought to draw from this anomaly, I should judge, is that consciousness is an independent fact which observes its own laws and goes its own way in the universe. The more perfect the behaviorist's theory, the more completely is he obliged to resign any effort to include this strange and superfluous fact in the system of what he calls "nature"; and he must refer all questions as to its origin and destiny to its own intrinsic laws. It becomes for him strictly supernatural. The death of the brain would have, on this showing, no bearing whatever on the future destiny of what we call the self.

But this comment is, of course, purely negative in its value. It aids simply to relieve our minds with regard to the confident foreclosure of the question by those illogical logicians who are most emphatic in foreclosing it. We proceed to consider other logical obstacles to a clear judgment of the problem.

Aside from the materialistic inference, which escapes its channel, the chief metaphysical premiss from which a no-survival conclusion is drawn is *our habitual monism*: the world is one—there is no "other world." If there is no other world, there is no locus for departed spirits, since they obviously have no place in this world (unless through some metempsychosis, which we also omit from the argument). Objections to other-worldliness are moral as well as structural; the social ethic and the humanistic religion of our day alike insist that the salvation of the soul and of the world shall take place in the present scene of things, and form a part of the business of human history. This point will concern us later. For the present we are interested only in the concept of "otherness."

The imaginations of those who first conceived survival had no difficulty with the location of the other life or lives. It was in some far away place, some Heaven above the stars, some Western Paradise, some realm of Osiris or of Hades underneath the earth. Transit to these places implied a journey of the soul, a perilous passage, with strange mental transformations to be sure, but nevertheless a *motion*, like that of a physical body: and motion can never get beyond the given universe of space and time—the other life was still in some part of this universe. With growing astronomical sophistication, the pious let their minds dwell on the possibilities of other planets for the habitations of the soul. The modes of conveyance thither might be magical, but the regions were well within "Nature."

None of these conceptions is any longer possible. If there is another life, there must be another Nature. And if there is but one space-time order, there can be but one Nature: for Nature is defined as the system of all events in the space-time universe. The word "other" is treacherous. It is properly applicable to anything which is partial: for any object with a boundary, there may be another such. But when applied to the unbounded whole of things, the word "other" loses its meaning: we seem to ourselves to mean something by the phrase "other world" only by illicitly drawing an imaginery boundary about this world. So runs the thought of the monist.

This thought is bound up with a certain conception of space. According to this conception, the space we inhabit is complete after its own kind, and being complete must be unique: for since it occupies (or rather, is) all the room there is, there is no "outside" in which another space could deploy its elements. To put the matter technically, we may think of the "whole of space" as the totality of positions which would be swept by an expanding sphere centered at a given point and moving outward without

limit. It may also be defined as the totality of positions
which could be reached from a given point by continuous
motion, or which are related to a given point by distance
and direction. But if one point, A, can be reached from
another point, B, then B can be reached from A: hence
every point in space will serve as well as any other as a
center—each will define the same totality. If we were to
try to define two different spaces by starting from remote
points we should only define the same space.

By this same reasoning, if we were to attempt to define
two or more coexisting "spaces," they would have to be so
related as to have *no point in common*. Nor could one be
outside the other; for "outsideness" is a spatial relationship, i.e., a relation between two fragments of the same
space which have no points in common. If, then, there is
to be an "other" space, it is necessary (and also sufficient)
to define a point which is not related to any point in the
given space by distance and direction. It is natural to
assume that no such point can be defined, and hence that
there is no other space.

This was Kant's point of view. He was deeply impressed
with the notion of an object whose character was such
that there could be but one instance of it, and that instance complete and infinite. His wonder was justified. It
is true that modern mathematics is accustomed to speak
of spaces in the plural. It speaks of spaces of different
type. Euclidean and non-Euclidean; it speaks also of
plural instances of space of the same type. Each such
space is complete; yet no one of them need have a point
in common with any other. This freedom in setting up
spaces is derived from the play of imagination in setting
up alternative sets of postulates from which various algebras of geometry may be drawn. Modern mathematics

makes no assumption that there is more than one actual or real space: its plural spaces are imaginary.

Nevertheless, it is important for our purposes that the imagination can deal with plural spaces. We are concerned solely with the possible meaning of a relation, that of "otherness" as applied to space. If mathematics can make a significant transition from one space to another, that transition may afford the relation we seek.

For the mathematician, the transition is obviously a mental one. Each of his spaces is set up by an act of thought. The passage from one to another is a shift of attention. Thus points in one of his spaces if they are re-lated at all to points in another are certainly not spatially related: they are related solely by way of this common mental origin. There is no more meaning in asking how far a point in one space is from a point in another, than in asking how far the stream in the picture is from the floor of the room in which the picture is hung. The two problems are precisely similar; for art has been long in advance of mathematics in devising a plurality of spaces as the regions for a plurality of worlds which neither inter-penetrate nor interfere, though each is infinite and com-plete. The catastrophes of the drama have no tendency to shake the house in which the drama is shown: the transi-tions from world to world are mental, not spatial nor causal.

And dream, in turn, has been in advance of art. For in dream, the space-time world in which events take place need have no point in common with the space-time world of waking life. The structure of the dream world presents this interesting difference from that of the work of art: that in art, the self as observer or maker remains outside of the thing made and conscious of its otherness from the "real" world, whereas in dream the self is an actor to whom the waking world is for the moment nonexistent (except in the rare occasions in which one knows that one is dreaming) and the transition to and from dream is involuntary. The catastrophes of the dream world fortunately leave the real world unshaken; though the reverse is not the case, the "otherness" is not complete. But the structural relations, the intramental transition from world to world, present the logical qualities which may enable us, as they enabled primitive men, to use the notion of an "other" world without confusion.

So far, we pursue the purely logical aspect of the notion of another life in another world. It is not the province of logic to deal with the concrete aspects of any problem: these lie before us. While we thus recur to the comment that such arguments as these leave on the mind an unbanishable sense of triviality, since the issues of life and death are not here, we may fairly remind ourselves that the issues of life are issues of thought, and that thought is often halted by unnecessary obstacles—not less in our day than in earlier days, but, I fancy, more so, since we live more consciously by thought and less by instinct. And while many of these issues are trivial, we may remember with humility that they are not the difficulties of the simple but of instructed and ingenious minds. It is for the sake of the intelligent that we must be momentarily logicians.

THE MIND AND ITS BODY

There is one further preliminary issue, not purely logical but turning on a point of logic, which has such wide influence and is so involved in natural sophistry that we may give it separate treatment. It is the question of the relation of mind and body. Common judgment on the question of survival is, I think, more governed by this than by any other observation, that "mind and body vary together," an observation which every extension of knowledge confirms and makes more precise.

I use a certain latitude in calling this thesis an observation, for we never perceive the two in process of varying together. In the sense in which we perceive the body, we do not perceive the mind at all: mental changes in other people we infer from bodily changes—the co-variation is not so much a result as an assumption. But having assumed it, in momentary transactions, the idea confirms itself in the large, and we accept the broad agreement of physical life cycle with mental life cycle as a theorem so stable that to question it discounts the judgment of the questioner. And on the basis of this theorem, death is death, as final for mind as for brain.

On this point we are all scientists, and would have little interest in an ancient issue between the scientific and the poetic type of mind, if it were not for the genius of an ancient poet which may still have its logical instruction. For Plato, the soul could have but one body at a time, but in different lives might be tenant of a series of different bodies. Aristotle, the scientist, was rightly disturbed by the nonchalance with which Plato allowed the soul not only to change bodies, but even to become released from any body and to wander through the nether regions bodiless and glad, as if freed from an encumbrance and also from an enemy of clear thought and good morals. Against such irresponsible imagining, Aristotle brought forward the impressive thesis that the distinction between soul and body is an abstraction: they are working parts of the same being; the soul is nothing but the living principle of the given body, and therefore inconceivable apart from it.

Aristotle differed from the modern physiologist in holding that the converse is also true; the body is inconceivable apart from its mind. When we think of an organic body by itself we have to ascribe to it a "capacity for life": the *psyche* is simply the "entelechy" or realization of that capacity. Without it the body does not operate, does not live, and is therefore not truly a body. And the soul, in turn, is as unintelligible apart from a specific body whose life it is, as breathing is unintelligible apart from a specific lung, or vision apart from a specific eye.

On this view, the body is not the residence of a separable tenant, still less a prison house or hindrance to moral aspiration: it is that which alone gives the soul a reason for being, a footing in the universe. And each particular soul is the completion of a particular body, and could fit no other. That the soul of a man should appear in the body of a fox or a lion is only a shade more absurd than that the soul of Caesar should appear in the body of Mussolini. Aristotle would have relished the problem of a seventeenth-century Harvard thesis: Whether the speech of Baalam's ass involved a temporary alteration of the animal's vocal chords.

On this issue, modern thought has gone wholly Aristotelian. In doing so it has turned up a puzzle from which Aristotle was free. For Aristotle who was happily ignorant of the precise functions of the brain—thinking of it as a sort of cooling device for the superheated humors of the body—avoided the embarrassment of having two agencies controlling the same events. We happen to know what the brain is for, at least in part, namely, the higher coordination of behavior. But if we know what our minds

are for, they also appear to be engaged in the higher coordination of behavior. We thus have two entities doing
the same thing: *what my brain does, I do!* We seem to
have a duplicate and equivalent control. This anomalous
situation we seek to escape either by identifying the two
entities—the brain *is* the mind—or by denying that the
control apparently exercised by the mind is real. Aristotle
would have been obliged to reject both alternatives, for
there were two matters on which he was completely certain:
(1) that the brain is not the mind, and (2) that the mind
is the real activity-pattern of the body. But these convictions imply that Aristotle, with all his vast common sense,
and his remarkable insight into the functional union of
soul and body, has no solution for the modern problem;
for this problem is made by what we know of the brain.
On the other hand, the modern scientist has no solution
which will provide for those two things that Aristotle
knew. This is the impasse which the problem has come to
in our time, leading many thinkers to attempt an escape
from the problem by redefining mind and body.

It is here that we have to make our logical observation.
Little as we actually know of the physiological basis of
mental life, there is no good reason for doubting any of
the surmises that lead to the quandary of "duplicate control." Whatever I seem to myself to do, when I direct my
body to do this and that—all of this can be theoretically
referred to brain events without remainder. We need not,
however, assume that these two controls are identical: we
may say either that these brain events are the faithful and
complete *image* of my mental events, or that my mental
events are the faithful and complete *image* of the brain
events. Either way of putting it satisfies the Aristotelian
doctrine of the exact and unique fitness between a given

mind and a given body. But the first way of putting it—
that the brain events, without being identical with the
mental events, are an exact image of them in another
medium—frees us from the inference that to one mind
there is one and only one body, and admits us (with prudent reserves) into the cosmos of Plato.

For note that the condition required by the postulates
of physiological psychology—that the brain events shall
perfectly correspond, one-to-one, with events passing in
the mind—can be met *by a whole class of bodies*—not by
one body alone. Consider a face mirrored in a series of
mirrors: each is the precise reflection of this face and no
other, yet each reflection is numerically distinct from
every other. Imagine these mirrors slightly curved, and
each curved with a slight difference from every other: we
shall then have a series of reflections, each slightly and
differently distorted—qualitatively as well as numerically
different, yet each one recognizable as the image of this
face and no other. Or let your hand cast a series of
shadows, as the light takes different positions; each
shadow differs from every other, and yet each shadow is
the shadow of your hand, and could be the shadow of no
other hand and of no other object under heaven.

The mathematician has no difficulty in expressing the
principle of this remark. B, the brain event, corresponds
precisely with C, the conscious event; that is, B is a function of C. But B is also a function of something else, let
us say, the environment, E. Then for any one value of C,
there will be as many possible values of B as there are
possible values of E. Without violating the Aristotelian
principle of exact correspondence, but because of it, the
same mind, C, in a different environment, E′, would necessarily have a different brain event, B′, and so, in sum, a

different body. Thus to a given mind there would correspond a *class* of possible bodies, and not one only. This class might possibly be infinite.

We may recur at this point to our illustration of the dream—from which the superstitious mind of the race has taken too much of the content of its metaphysics, while the unsuperstitious, repelled by this abuse, have almost wholly neglected its instructive logical structure. The dreaming person has a dream world, but also a dream body: his awareness of this body is usually much more obscure than his awareness of the environing objects, but he is frequently conscious of bodily effort, and of power or lack of power to act in definite ways, some of which (as flying) are characteristically different from those of the waking state. This dream body is thus "another" body than the waking body, somewhat in the sense imagined by Plato, while yet conforming strictly to the principle of unique fitness to the individual mind insisted upon by Aristotle.

Our divergence from Aristotle lies in this point: that he seems to have considered the body as the primary reality in point of genesis, out of which the *psyche* emerges as the perfecting function, somewhat as reason supervenes in the developing human being; whereas in the view here stated the *psyche* is the original reality, and the body-and-brain system is its derivative or representation within the natural context. But for Aristotle also, the *psyche* is said to be the substance of the man, and the perfection of a thing its true "nature"; hence the apparent divergence may be merely a symptom of the fact that for Aristotle many of our problems of mind and body had not attained the sharpness which they have had in modern times, especially since the work of the great Distinguisher, Descartes.

So far for our logical preliminaries, which have aimed solely to release from prevailing fog certain conceptions without which the idea of survival cannot so much as be defined. We now turn to consider certain broad characters of the structure of experience which bear concretely on the problem.

IV

A DILEMMA
OF WORLD STRUCTURE

WE cannot today begin an inquiry into the general structure of the cosmos with the words "mind" and "body," or, "subject" and "object," or, "the self" and "the physical world," as pairs of terms already well understood, of which we have only to discover the true relationship. For common usage we understand these terms well enough; for meeting a persistent puzzle, we have reason to suspect them of concealing an ancient trap. We must try to define them; the effort to do so drives us to new starting points—more elementary notions in terms of which these conceptions can be built up.

For example, the physical object, the "thing," is the commonest coin of the world's thinking and of its vocabularies. It is an object which everybody can observe and which is not altered—perceptibly—by the operation of looking at it, nor by the light that falls on it. Nevertheless, in all strictness, we are not seeing the object, but the object-modified-by-light-and-by-our-proximity-and-by-our-instrument-of-vision. What we actually have is a perception into whose make-up numerous factors have entered, and from it we have "constructed" that object which

seems to stand before us in its own character. We need
a less committed starting point.

It is natural that such a starting point should be sought
in "immediate experience"; for where else than in experience can we find the raw stuff of meanings which are simple
and inescapable? Interpretations of experience I may
doubt: I cannot doubt the fact that I have it, and that
such and such contents are present. Thus physics today,
troubled by inconsistencies among its hypotheses, is more
willing than usual to give a hearing to "sense data" as
possible sources for its logical simples.

This starting point is especially convenient for describ-
ing phenomena which are relative to the observer and his
instruments; and there are physicists who, regarding all
phenomena as thus relative, are prone to identify the
scope of the world with the scope of experience. But "experience" (in spite of all effort to keep it neutral as between the mind which experiences and the objects which
it experiences) remains tarred with a subjective and private quality. From such a starting point, one has to labor
to construct those simple notions with which physical
science habitually begins, such as "the physical object,"
"other minds," "verifiability." For this reason many
physicists prefer the risks of beginning with the physical
object as a simple idea, and introducing corrections for
the relativities of observation and instrument.

We have then at least two different scientific languages
constructed on two diverse sets of primitive ideas. If these
languages were perfect instruments of inquiry they should
be precisely equivalent: we should have the same description of the world in each case, though in other words. In
practice this exact equivalence is not the case. And the
differences become critical at a point which concerns our

present inquiry—the place of the mind or the self in nature.

According to the language which begins with the physical object—the language of "physicalism"—everything can be readily provided for except the mind. The presence or absence of consciousness in connection with an animal organism cannot be verified, and the theoretical picture would be cleaner if it were omitted. The human organism is a part of the natural world. It arises out of nature; while it lives, the lines of causation from all surrounding nature run through it; it goes back to nature. The mind which accompanies it will follow the same course: for it also, the world which surrounds the organism surrounds it; this world existed before its advent and will continue after its disappearance. From this point of view, *the self is within the world.*

According to the other language—that which begins with sense data, the subjective language—everything can be readily provided for except a real physical world. This language has no use for the concepts of substance or causality: it is not concerned with the ultimate nature of matter or energy. *Its* theoretical picture is cleaner if *these* are omitted. The world of nature is a mental construct falling within the whole of "experience." My direct sense data, to be sure, touch but a small part of this physical world: but it is my thought which spins out, from these occasional and almost accidental materials of sense perception, a continuous world; and it is my hypotheses which make its changes intelligible and consistent. Its fabric is thus through and through mental: and for this language, accordingly, *the world is within the self.*

Between these two views, arising from different languages, logic has no criterion for choosing. And physical science (not being concerned with the destiny of the conscious self) has no preference between them, so long as its own accepted range of phenomena are equally well provided for. The physical language remains for it the more usual. But it can accustom itself also to the subjective language which, after all, only reverts to a remark of Aristotle to the effect that "the *psyche* is, in a sense, everything that exists. For whatever exists is an object either of sensation or of thought; and objects of sensation and thought are, in a way, identical with the sensation and thought themselves." [1] At this point Aristotle trembles on the verge of saying that the world is, "in a sense," within the *psyche*!

But while logic cannot choose between the languages, and science declines to choose except on grounds of convenience, the common man can hardly retain such a perfect poise. He understands what is meant by a purely linguistic difference; and yet he has a suspicion that between a language for which the self is in the world and a language for which the world is in the self there may be conveyed—by a metaphysical innuendo of which the logician is not wholly guiltless—material differences which concern his own fate. This suspicion is confirmed if he follows these two positions to some of their corollaries:

If, as the language of physicalism has it, the self is within the world, then the self is finite in space and time, and there may be many such selves in the world wholly separate from and "outside of" one another. If the world is within the self, then it would appear to follow that the world is finite—not in space and time, but as an aspect of experience; and the corresponding conclusion would

[1] *De Anima* III, c. viii. Wheelwright's translation.

follow that there may be for the self many such worlds—
a somewhat startling conclusion, for which our logical
preliminaries have prepared us.

If the self is within the world, the death of the self is
also an event within the one world, and as much a mark of
the temporal finitude of the self as its birth: there is nothing of the self beyond that boundary. If the world is
within the self, death as an event within the world has no
necessary value as a time boundary of the self.

In view of these divergent corollaries, the common man
is inclined to reject the invitation to regard these differences as purely linguistic, and to take it that he ought to
choose between the proposed modes of expression as if
they were differences of metaphysic. They remind him of
an antithesis in the history of philosophy: that between
idealism and realism, in which until recently, men were
called upon to take sides. To the idealist, the typical item
of reality was just this element of "experience" which
Descartes called a thought, Locke an idea, Hume an impression, the logical analyst a sense datum. To the realist,
the typical item of reality was just this element of nature
which we call a physical thing. The logician of today protests that he is deliberately refusing to talk about "realities," doubting whether that word has any assignable
meaning. The plain man remembers that the word "reality" had just those functional meanings with which he is
now concerned—the "real" was understood to be that
which endures, that which corrects errors, that which explains appearances: and under whatever name, it seems
to him a highly concrete issue whether one ascribes these
properties to the sort of thing we call a thought or to the
sort of thing we call a quantum of energy.

And since neither the logician nor the scientist is willing to deal with this question, and he is obliged to deal with it himself, it occurs to the plain man to ask whether this indifference of the technicians, expressed in the form, "Either language is admissible," may be translated for his own concreter interests into the form, *"Both views of reality are true."*

For, he reflects, there is a sense in which the brick or the atom or the ultimate physical unit is the standard of reality. When he considers his own consciousness in its variable, flickering, vulnerable character, he would aspire to be as real as a stone post or as a law of nature. Since he comes out of that natural world, he must draw his reality from it; and aware of continuous dependence upon it, he is impelled to say "I am only as real as my world."

But there is also a sense in which his thoughts and feelings are the standard of reality. Since Descartes, no one can put thought out of the list of real entities. When we speak of the "reality of a thing," we are aiming at its "true inwardness," the way it feels to itself: and if, as an inanimate thing it has no way of feeling to itself, we rightly judge it a relatively empty sort of being. Nothing of this empty sort, though it be the stone post itself, can be as real as an experience of joy or suffering. If in a storm at sea one considers which is more real, the tempest or the agonized heaving of men at the pumps, one may very well yield the physical issue to the winds, and still judge that the intensities of feeling within those laboring human frames are the realest entities in the situation. Seeing this, one grasps the other standard: "My world, at best, can be only as real as I am." It derives its accent of actuality from the circumstance that I am conscious of it.

Thus in the ordinary acknowledgments of thought, the

standard of reality passes from object to subject and back again; neither of these modes of judgment is to be rejected; the standard must somehow be twofold and the truly concrete and durable being, the "real," must include both.

But how is this to be understood? The plain man gains some light when he tries to carry through the subjective view of things, according to which the world is within the self. What does this world, which is alleged to be within me, itself contain? Among other things, it contains organisms and their careers, and the selves connected with them, just as the opposing view of physicalism would have it. With the other selves, it includes also *my* self! Then the self, in containing nature, contains the self—in another aspect. Then, becoming suddenly self-conscious, he exclaims, "That is the plain fact of the case! I, the observer, in surveying my world am also looking on at myself as an observed fact within my world. The effort to know the world of objects brings me to a new mode of self-consciousness, a knowledge of myself which I might not otherwise attain. The dilemma I have been struggling with is now traced to a doubleness in the meaning of my 'self': in whatever sense I contain my world, in that sense I also contain myself. It is I who am a twofold being, and yet in both aspects the same self."

In this way the plain man has lighted upon a principle which, if we are right, will have far-reaching consequences for his views of life and death, as well as of other matters. We shall call it the *principle of "empirical duality"*—a phrase shortly to be explained. It is not the simple and ancient paradox of the static self-consciousness, but an experience which develops out of self-consciousness and presents the self in a twofold relationship to other beings.

The plain man is relieved by this insight from the sense of contradiction which has been dogging him; but the logical difficulty is not abolished—it is transferred to the complexity of his own nature, whither we shall now attempt to follow it.

V

THE PRINCIPLE OF DUALITY

THE SELF AND THE SUBCONSCIOUS

ONE who is seeking light on the nature of the self might naturally turn for help to the science of psychology. What account does it give of these two aspects of the self? It is disconcerting to learn that contemporary psychology is in doubt whether it can do anything with even one aspect of the self, not to mention two.

There is good reason for this doubt. For psychology, as a science, has to occupy itself with objects which can be identified, such as sensations, thoughts, feelings or their physical expressions. Such objects might be designated as states or contents of a self; but this reference to a self would hardly aid in identifying them unless the self could serve as an identifiable object. But the self is not one of these contents: there is no sensation of the self. The phrase "a visual sensation" may be equivalent to the phrase "I see"; but this "I" is a constant factor in all such experiences, and is therefore of no distinctive use in the theory of vision. It can be understood as present without being continually repeated. To say that several states belong to the same self is another way of saying that they occur *together*; for how could they occur together except in the same mind? Hence empirical psychology tends to dispose of the self in the simple assumption that certain mental states are together with others.

Some psychologists recognize that this is not wholly adequate to the facts; for the self appears to be active; it is not merely a place of assemblage for its several "contents." What does it do? It makes a difference in the way these contents cohere, get associated, attended to, emphasized or forgotten. It is like an invisible wind which selects, retains, discards; or like a magnetic field—also invisible—which shows its effect in the way a scattering of iron filings arrange themselves. But these activities—if they are such—may again be disposed of by descriptive psychology as contents, so to speak, of the second order, under such names as "attention," "disposition," "active set." They call for no reference to an imperceptible agent, the self; for what the science is concerned with is the events, not the agent; the changes, not the hypothetical and constant source of change.

In these ways, for empirical psychology, the self within the world tends to lose that significant unity which it has for the plain man instituting the inquiry. And as for that other aspect of the self whose language takes the form, "The world is within the self," this self is nowhere recognized. It resembles too much, perhaps, that grammatical subject, that "I" of the phrase, "I think," which Kant called the transcendental unity of apperception, and which (he averred) could by its very definition as subject never be an empirical object. We cannot ask a psychology, bent on achieving status as a natural science, to deal with any self (if it does so much) except the self which is an object within nature.

But it is just at this point that the plain man is likely

to insist that the inclusive self he is talking about *is empirical*, though to perceive it may require a shift in the angle of vision. And in support of this view we may now put forward a thesis, namely, that there are empirical elements of self-consciousness, and that the omission of them has revenged itself in one of the maladroit chapters of modern psychology, the confused and fumbling theory of the *subconscious*. For, in my judgment, the various alleged contents and functions of the subconscious are for the most part fragments of this inclusive self.

If we ask what the subconscious is supposed to contain we find it presented to us as a sort of cellar to which miscellaneous rejected states of mind are relegated. It is the residence of uneasy ghosts of repressed memories; also of furtive primitive impulses arising from animal heredity and vainly striving for the recognition of overt consciousness.

A very different group of contents is the mass of traces of past experience, forgotten or remembered and not being referred to, the body of "memory" and of the undistinguished experiences from which one has learned, such as that dim recollection of once-burned fingers which has long continued to modify subsequent impulses to grasp flames. Of this forever accumulating multitude of shades for which we may still conveniently use the term "apperceptive mass," we may say that we are not thinking *of* it chiefly because we are always thinking *with* it. Every incident of our lives passes into it; and whether or not we ever single out a given incident for individual recall—though we never again think of it—we shall continue to think *with* it until we die. Its presence in memory, or in subconsciousness, is anything but a condition of inactive storage; it is an active functioning in receiving, recognizing, evaluating every new experience.

When one says that "I" have met a new experience, it is evident that this "I" is a variable; for such experience is met well or ill, adequately or inadequately, somewhat in proportion to the equipment afforded by this ordered magazine of past experience: We begin thus to note the identity of the "self" and the "subconscious." And the same identity will appear as we consider two further groups of contents commonly assigned to the subconscious, the repressions and the possibilities.

Psychiatrists have accustomed us to the notion of a rill of unfavorable comment upon experience, persons, our own budding impulses—comment which while repressed is not annihilated but is said to persist in subconsciousness where it may work mischief, build up "complexes," incite obscure mental disorders. There is an abundance of clinical material which this scheme more or less fairly interprets; but there are certain obvious follies in the stage setting. For since repression is a conscious event and cannot be performed nor continued except by an awareness of what is being repressed: since it is "I" who act as censor, it is "I" who also entertain the rebellious comment; it is "I" whose wishes are always partly unfulfilled, and who persist in the hope that some day in some guise they may receive expression. An unconscious impulse is no impulse at all; a subconscious impulse, at least half-lighted by conscious attention, is *my* impulse, though I may hold it in leash until it can go with my full sanction.

Unsatisfied wishes (including our much-curbed pugnacities, impulses to criticize, condemn, denounce, fight, kill, destroy, held in check until we know what we want to do) merge with another group of subconscious contents not less important, but less noted—our undefined possibilities, sometimes referred to as our "powers." If one is asked point blank what his powers are, an instant introspection affords him little light. An adolescent boy has powers; he is aware of them as an *ensemble* in the sense that they contribute to his self-assurance; yet he would be at a loss to define them. He seldom thinks of them; he habitually thinks *with* them. He can hardly be aware of them as outlined facts because, for one reason, he has not learned their limits. Maturity brings much knowledge of the limits of specific powers—one's speed, capacity for figures, chess, music, professional prowess—but there remains an integral sense of power, inseparable from self-consciousness, to which no limit is ever drawn.

This unawareness of limit is sometimes referred to as the "infinitude" of the self. It is truer, I think, to regard it not as a positive or actual infinitude but as a *negative wholeness,* an absence of boundary, inhibition, division in regard to oneself. With the absence of boundary there goes the absence of explicit consciousness—the quality is subconscious, closely identified with self: we live in it as if we had a command of its whole nature. As in the familiar instance of space, whatever fragment we have rounds itself into an integral whole. Or, more concretely, in the case of vision: I do not see the effect of the blindspot in my eye as a blank in the field of vision, nor do I remark the line limiting that field. I do not positively assert the infinitude of the field, but the absence of definite limit allows it to assume a certain integrity and totality. So with our knowledge. Few human beings are inclined to assert omniscience; yet few confront the world originally as if there were anything there they could not understand.

Skepticism is a late acquisition of the race. It is Hobbes who adduces as evidence for the equality of mankind in respect to mentality that "every man is content with his share." Is it not the nature of knowing, to *know*? And all the difficulties it meets in this enterprise rather defer than cancel this original assurance: the studied and measured modesties of Hume and Kant leave it skeptical rather of them than of itself. It may be right! And so of the essence of other powers and qualities of the mind: it is not a positive infinitude or omnipotence which consciousness asserts of itself, it is a "negative wholeness." And since this general sense of potentiality is a part of that apperceptive mass with which one encounters every new task and situation, it is properly included in the content of the subconscious.

The various ingredients of subconsciousness which we have thus reviewed begin to exhibit, not a miscellany, but a quasi-organic character of pertinence one to another. It is active, selective attention which focuses consciousness on this and that object from the midst of a field of objects, thus throwing the greater part of the field into the "margin"; it is likewise an active, selective intention which focuses the trend of action and throws the rest of a thousand incipient impulses into the limbo of nonselected, perhaps repressed, ideas-of-action. But nothing can be discarded or repressed except for the sake of something taken as of greater worth for the purpose in hand. It is the "apperceptive mass" both of memory and of potentiality which is giving experience this structure: but this is only a more analytic way of saying that "I," as a felt system of powers and possibilities, attend, evaluate, choose, discard, both among my objects and among my impulses

toward those objects: *the ingredients of "subconsciousness" are empirical ingredients of myself*—of the self
which hovers over experience, the inclusive, observing and
judging self. This self, we may say, is subconscious to
itself; or conversely, what we call subconsciousness, so far
from being a sort of mental sub-basement, is at the center
of selfhood, and the invidious term "subconsciousness" is
an inept recognition of the fact that the primary springs
of selfhood are not habitually at the focus of its outgoing
interests.

Our chief concern here is to do away with those traves-
ties of the self which neglect its empirical aspects, or present them, as it were, in the flat—like a mural painting
spread out in one dimension, or like a "stream of consciousness" whose whole sense lies in the surface layer,
however it may be disturbed by irrelevant bubblings from
slimy depths below. Those older descriptions which presented the self as a "union of opposites" had at least the
advantage of recognizing that the self has depth and inner
duality—not merely factual superfice, dismissible in a
list of "contents." The self observes itself, judges itself,
directs itself, controls itself, places itself in the world; and
both as judging and as judged it is directly known to us.
We have now to indicate some of the bearings of this
empirical duality.

TRAITS OF THE TWO SELVES

For the sake of brevity, we may refer to the two aspects
of the self we have been distinguishing as two selves: the
self which is within the world, and the self which contemplates the world from a point not within the world, and in
this sense includes the world. We might designate these
two selves (invidiously) as the selves of the lower level

and of the upper level, or (inaccurately) as the observed
and the observing selves. We might better call them the
"excursive" and the "reflective" selves. The word "excursive" simply implies that the self-within-the-world is a
self of behavior, entangled in affairs; and that these
affairs have the value of excursions, in the sense that they
report their results back again to the center from which
the foray issued. If consciousness were a "stream" it
would go on and on with no attachments and no reissuings:
but as a series or system of excursions, each one launched
under a working hypothesis subject to revision, we understand that it has its returns, its incessant new beginnings
with equally incessant accumulation of meaning. The reflective self, behind scenes, is the constant judge, guide,
initiator of this excursive activity.

The self passes into the lower level, or into excursion,
in the process of "decision" of which we were speaking
earlier, whereby it becomes involved in dates, local circumstances and other irrelevant particulars. Each excursion,
under the aegis of a single decision, has a unity of its own,
its "idea." An "excursion" is a far more significant unit of
mental life than, let us say, a "sensation" or a "feeling";
it constitutes a paragraph of personal history, with an
integral time epoch of its own, long or short. The excursive self has thus a marked pluralism and discontinuity,
though the intricate pattern made by the overlapping of
numerous simultaneous excursions gives it the semblance
of an irregular, eddying flow. Meantime the reflective self
(recognizable as the self of detachment in our earlier discussion) is uninterrupted in its survey, maintaining its
own independence and reserve from the entanglements of
the attached, occupied and dated self: its cumulative
judgments of that self and of its reports contribute to the

building of that "apperceptive mass" which is its empirical substance.

The self has been called a "union of opposites"; we have already indicated that this tantalizing conception has one advantage—it is not a flat-wash conception of selfhood. Perhaps we may rescue this phrase from some of its obscurity and at the same time develop our notion of the self as a reflective-excursive system, by pointing out that the opposing qualities, which the self has been said to unite, tend to distribute themselves unequally to these two aspects or selves, now sufficiently distinguished.

Thus, the self is said to unite the *actual and the potential*; and this is true. Indeed, it is only in a self that an actual possibility can be found, and this only on the assumption that the self is "free," i.e., that the alternatives which appear before it in the moment of decision are real alternatives. In the process of decision, some of these possibilities disappear; one or more become "actualized." Hence the potential is the special province of the reflective self; the actual is the special province of the excursive and dated self.

In a similar way, the proposal that the self is a union of *finite and infinite* can be given an empirical meaning. The reflective self is infinite in the sense we have already indicated; it enjoys that "negative wholeness" which in various directions is unaware of limit. The excursive self has the accepted finitude of decision, which limits itself to the narrow field of possibility it intends to actualize; and its achievement has the finitude of every actual fact.

These contrasts are imperfectly outlined: I merely indicate them, and pass on to the antithesis which now chiefly concerns us. The self is said to be a union of *the temporal*

and the eternal; and again the statement is true, but in
need of interpretation. It may indicate to us that the
reflective self and the excursive self stand in different relations to time. This is a fact of experience; and here I feel
that our empirical psychology lags behind contemporary
physics in recognizing the inner complexity of our consciousness of time.

The excursive self, as we have said, is preeminently the
dated self. It is immersed in the time flow of the physical
environment with which it deals. Physics inclines to uti-
lize its sense of the present moment, its "now," to define
physical simultaneity of near-by events.

The reflective self experiences the time order as it does
the space order in a roomier fashion as an unbounded whole
within which the several time positions of excursive activity are placed, as also the whole arc of the excursion, its
beginning and end. The discontinuities of action are set in
an unbroken continuity, which is time itself. For the physical world and for the listening ear the fugue *is* fugitive;
its successive notes drop out of being as they arise. For
reflection the whole flight is felt at once, and it is possible
to take mental possession of its total course, without which
it has no meaning. Yet the character of temporal succession is not lost: on the contrary, unless elements of
succession were known together, there could be only a
flight of nows—succession itself would remain unknown.
This capacity to hold successive moments in consciousness
at once without losing their time spread is familiar to
philosophers—familiar as one of the standing wonders
of experience which still awaits satisfactory interpretation. The word "eternal" seems to me not alone unneces-
sarily baffling, but misleading, as though it were something in contrast with time, instead of what it is: the very

essence of the time order. For time can constitute an order only when its multitude of elements are taken as members of a class, held in one thought. For the reflective self, the time continuum is held as a single fact in "negative wholeness"—not as an actual infinitude, but without sense of beginning or end, at once. It takes no longer to contemplate a thousand years than to contemplate ten minutes: and yet—this is the miracle—each may be thought of in its true extent. In this sense, time is within the reflective self, whereas the dated self is in time. The reflective self is not timeless, nor out of time: it has its own acts of decision and moments of review which are dated: yet in a single act it pervades all time.

It is only for the self that time spreads itself out in its true character. For the physical world, the past is pure past—it was but is not—and the future is pure future. For the facts of memory and anticipation there is no physical analogue, not even in the brain: for present traces of past events are not remembrance. Nature makes its own records, such as the geologist reads in the rocks; they are completely devoid of temporal quality except for the mind that reads them—superposition is translated as laterness, etc. In complex structures there may be signs of wear which indicate, again to the reader, processes long continued. But in the ultimate ingredients of nature there can be no sign of wear: energy itself has no age. Imagine a perfect pendulum, frictionless, oscillating in a vacuum over a heavy body—a closed system alone in the universe: what would there be to distinguish the tenth oscillation from the ninth, or these from the ten-billionth? Nothing. It would be a clock without a record, devoid of every sign of its own duration, always *"herrlich, wie am ersten Tag!"* This agelessness of the ultimate physical facts is at once glorious and appalling: there is no time summation in the roots of nature. Entropy itself is ignorant of its own history. But for a being with a memory, items may accumulate and retain their distinctiveness and their place forever, without crowding, because the mental time order is a true additional dimension of being, not another of the simultaneous dimensions of space.

Remembrance is thus a veritable immortalization of events which would otherwise be gone. Their endurance is conferred, and conferred by the reflective self. The monuments we earlier referred to as physical aids to the memory of the dead, are indeed less fragile than the human organism in the ordinary physical environment; but in themselves they are present facts, commemorating nothing: they are but parts of a circuit by which memory aids itself to its own goal. Memory is not an automatic, mechanical, indifferent retention of everything that strays into experience. Just as attention fixes on what is significant now, so memory fastens on what may be significant hereafter, both pleasant and unpleasant experiences. Thus the self builds its own history, and the contours of this individual past remain plastic, as its estimates of value vary: under a newly conceived distaste, treasured episodes may be relegated to the indistinguishable mass, old prides may be rejected by a new shame, and former shames lift up their heads with arrived self-confidence. Deeds are irrevocable; the past is irrevocable, but the immortalizations of memory remain subject to an altering—presumably improving—judgment of what is fit to endure.

It is not enough, in view of all this, to say that the reflective self "surveys" time, or perceives it as an independent object. Time is, to be sure, an objective character of the world; but it is a character which reaches no totality except in reflective selfhood. This raises the surmise that the reflective self is involved in the being of time, and is therefore durable in its own nature.

The excursive self is transitional, intentionally time limited, a passage aware of its own transit. The reflective self in observing the time flow distinguishes itself from that flow, but also continues through it. The excursive self is not alone a system of finite time flights: it is subject to lapses, breaches, interruptions; it flickers, wanders, goes out during sleep, resumes life on waking not by any grace of its own but by grace—it seems—of more reliable bodily processes which mend and bridge the abandoned continuities. But why is this self, upon waking, the *same self?* Is it indeed because of the faithfulness of the physical world it deals with? Is it because this body and these walls are the same body and the same walls as yesterday? But the body and the walls of yesterday are gone: the body is indeed the same, but it is wholly incapable of presenting the self with the knowledge of that fact—it can work in the moment, it cannot retain its own past. It is the self which recognizes its body as the same; the physical constancy would be meaningless were it not for the underlying constancy of memory. And its self-recognition is dependent far less on these its physical loyalties than on a deeper loyalty, namely, to its own interests and problems. The problem to which I awake this morning is not "similar" to the one I laid down last night: it is the identical problem, and will remain the same until the solution is found, through years if need be, over whatever gaps and absences of consciousness. This problem remains the same because I remain the same: it is "my" problem. And since a life span may be considered as the course of a single problem unremittingly pursued, the reflective self has an empirical duration at least as long. The subconscious self does not relax its hold on time. And it has resources to hold the excursive self to its own identity: if in years past I have made a promise, and performance is now due, the reflective self may acknowledge the debt, and in so doing establish the moral identity of selfhood underneath a thousand changes. The reflective self administers the time dimension both for the excursive self and for its world of nature.

We have been witnessing in our own day a renewed contest between two ancient philosophies, the philosophy of substance and the philosophy of flux, and on the whole the flux philosophy has come to dominance. To this view—which found a preliminary voice in Hume—the self figures as the shining example of a dethroned substance. As the substance of a physical object has been replaced by reliable laws of co-existence and change, so the substance of self has been replaced by laws of squence among mental contents, or by a principle of transmission in which, instead of true memory we have a perennially reconstituted atmosphere of inheritance.

This polemic has been an aid to clarity. We are well rid of that material pellet which lurked under the shell of the substantial "soul." But the newer philosophies of flux have also to be superseded. What we are now witnessing is the passing of both types, and their displacement by a truer account of change and endurance than can be given by either. If the substance philosophers have unconsciously worshiped a stone, the flux philosophers have been unintentional worshipers of death—for when change is ultimate, death becomes permanent.

The flux philosophy has been fascinated by the spurts and starts and flickerings of the dated self; and abetted by the incompleteness of empirical psychology has been ready to assume that the self has no account to give of its own persistences. It has not noticed that it is the *self which observes its own flickering*, which it could not do unless it also possessed a stabler mode of being, such as we are now finding in the reflective self. Unless there is something deeper than flux, flux can never know its own being.

We have one more opposition to record. The reflective self is a creative self and the dated self is its creature.

In all decision there is a possibility to be realized by way of some deed which affects the objective patterns of things. But also in all decisions there lurks an image—commonly a vaguer image—of a possible self which is being achieved. I choose to enter medicine, I choose to be a physician: what I do and what I become are inseparable. Jules de Gaultier suggested in his *Bovarysme* that we are all bent on becoming what we are not and have no native gift for being—attracted perversely by the unreachable. In which bit of extravagance there is this truth, that we find out what it is in us to be, in part by attempting many roles for which we have no gift, until this self of unlimited self-confidence, instructed by its excursions, discovers whom it *can be*, and aims to become that person.

Self-consciousness we have, as a momentary structural fact of experience; but the completion of self-consciousness is the task of a lifetime, and the general principle holds that we best understand that which we have made. Through the increments of countless decisions, the self which I become is the self which I can understand and objectify because I have been largely its maker. It is "I," as nearly as I can put myself into this medium—yet, as a product, it is somewhat other than my self. It is, let us say, the best version of myself I can now achieve, within this context and at this date; I have stuck by the original canvas; it is marred by erasures and new beginnings; I cannot pretend it a full success; of the infinitude of possibility I have dreamed, the unrealized exceeds what has been brought into being. The finite drawn out from the unlimited leaves the unlimited. Yet it has been a life to do it.

With these distinctions in mind between the two selves which constitute our working human self—the reflective self, which is (relatively) potential, infinite, time-inclusive, time-continuous, creative; the excursive self, which is (relatively) actual, finite, time-limited, time-discontinuous, created—we may now return to review the meanings of death.

VI

FURTHER MEANINGS
OF DEATH

In our earlier view of the meanings of death we re-marked how there may grow through the normal courses of living an individual willingness to die and a capacity for the renunciation of life. There remained a mystery in that willingness: it is irrational if death means the extinction of the subject of consciousness. It raised a doubt whether the human individual were realizing all he renounced or whether he were still blinded by his instinctive adoption of the social view of his passing.

We can now see the basis for that doubt. It is a simple matter to contemplate one's death. But when one does so, one does it *as a survivor*! Within oneself there is reproduced an element of social objectivity: it is the inclusive or reflective self which contemplates the death of the dated, excursive self, and is half able to accept it. The self does not contemplate nor know how to contemplate its own extinction. It can define itself as not being or as ceasing to be; but it remains the definer, unable to abandon itself in the meaning of those words, and unable to realize what an experience of coming to an absolute end might be. There could be no such experience. For to know that "This is the end" one must already see beyond that end, and know that there is nothing there: to assert, "I now die" is either an anticipation or a guess whose truth would be an accident. To gather the meaning of extinction one must both vanish and continue to be; the effort to realize death results in a sharpened awareness of that duality within self with which we have been dealing.

In our first thoughts about death we were in effect making use of that duality. The question is now raised whether the inclusive self could be reasonably conceived as a surviving self; and what, under such a view, the further meaning of death may be.

In any case, death remains death.

For any self, death must be an interruption—a break at an arbitrary point, so far as the self can see. If there is never sufficient reason for ending a conversation, still less can there be sufficient reason for the simultaneous cutting of all the strands of a human career. The best-concluded life is unprepared at the moment, is checked in the swing of an arm, in the flow of a pen, in the unraveling of a new-seen puzzle, in the training of a child. It is the destiny of the dated self not to be completed at any moment—that half-painted picture, that unfinished symphony, that partly-plowed field, that deserted campaign, that almost grasped idea! These are the broken edges of history, left forever as futurist images of action-going-on . . . and in so far truer to the living self than the repose of a patly concluded task, too much like the eternalized image of Lot's wife congealed in an attitude of retrospect.

What is thus broken off must be relinquished. But if the dated self is gone, is there in the reflective self any greater capacity for life? Is it by itself a complete being, or is it like one of those indestructible nonentities of the older Platonism or of the classical idealistic fancy? A merely subconscious, reflective, judging self with none of those characters of individuality, sensation, body, objects, empirical undertakings, conversation, would be as little of a person as a pure transcendental ego. The reflective self after all is but one aspect of a vital division of labor, and means little or nothing apart from its more empirical partner.

The answer depends on noting that the reflective self is something more than this name implies; potentiality is as near to its essence as contemplation; it is an unlimited nest of possibilities hardly broached, and a capacity to bring them into particular existence. We have spoken of it as creative and also as free. One's view of survival turns on what these too-fluent terms mean in one's philosophy.

The freedom of decision has sometimes been pictured as a sort of mechanical coin-flipping to lend an arbitrary overweight to one of two balanced alternatives. This is as poor a version of decision as could well be conceived. The self, in deliberating, is not occupied with a common stock of conventional alternatives. Bach's music was not eternally laid up in heaven, and extracted by him from an endless store of pre-existing musical ideas: it was not so much as *possible* until Bach conceived it. This idle idea of an infinite grab bag of eternal possibilities, from which finite deciders draw now a red ball, now a white, as pleases their fancy, assumes that no finite mind does more than reproduce and give flesh to a few of the infinite multitude of an eternal repertoire of universals: but the human will is not engaged in mere duplication. The field of alternative possibilities into which the self looks is first of all a field stocked by its own imagination, derived from a thousand sources and yet in every line its own product. It is impossible for two minds to contemplate the same concrete alternatives, though they be given the same names; for to each mind the alternatives become at once "what I can make of them." The world in which the deliberating mind operates is an "other" world with its own space-time order; it intends to superpose this imagined world, when its conception is satisfactory, upon the "actual" world, and in the act of decision construct a perfect splice! It confers actuality upon the dream of its own making. Thus Bach adds to the universe, when he pens his music, something which without his invention the universe would not have had and something which God himself had never thought. Thus the reflective self, drawing its hints from the experience of a multitude of excursions, gives back to history always more than it receives. And the self which it makes is a self which it alone has conceived.

If this account of decision is true, the terms freedom and creativity applied to human action have a certain literal force. The self gives actuality to possibilities; and *it has first made these possibilities.* Within the limits of its own conceiving and doing it is as real as what otherwise exists in the world. It would presumably remain something, and viable, even if the dated self it had built were obliterated. Death would then have a further meaning:

Death would mean, for the reflective self, the birth of its child, the dated self, and separation from it—release from its growing burden.

That child it leaves, in one sense dying in the moment of birth, in another sense the permanent possession of this present fabric of history. That individual is completed, fills its personal name with the meaning it will always carry, has a social continuance in the ramifying delta of its effects, vicariously enjoys that immortality of works and of remembrance which many would substitute for personal survival.

But death would also mean the persistence of the maternal prowess of the reflective self within which lie germs of other gestations.

Hence it would not necessarily mean loss of individuality, nor of sensation, nor of body, nor of objects. For in this creativity of the reflective self there lies the possibility of relation to other worlds which are also actual worlds. The self, in its freedom, is always standing as the bridge of connection between plural space-time orders. One of these is pre-eminently "actual," though it has no monopoly of reality: it is actual because it is the space-time world of a certain group of fellow selves, with whom this self is now in active intercourse by way of "this" nature, and "this" body. This group of fellow selves need not be the only such group in the universe, defining by their interplay a particular "world of nature." If there are other such groups, the death of this dated self would mean the severance of connection with this particular group of selves; it would conceivably be the occasion for beginning connection with another group.

Death would then mean the withdrawal of an insertion, the crumbling of a system of intercourse, the cessation of receptivity to this particular outer world. It might well mean reversion to a moment of latent being, a period of transition—since the transitions from world order to world order are intramental—reaching out for new pertinency and new belonging. And presumably the otherness to which the instinctive groping of the nuclear self would reach would be not simply moreness of such as one has had, but the dawning as well of new types of being, and of deeper categories of thought into which such modes of living as this may be involuted and understood with a more adequate power of knowing.

The acquired power to see life as a whole and the dated self as an object distinct from myself, which living brings, brings also the power to conceive a radical "otherness" in the universe. Death completes the meaning of the term "this" as applied to this life and this self; and therewith a possible other is given its completest meaning. There are shallow "others" in abundance scattered throughout experience—other places, other tasks, other persons, other ideas; but death unless it is an end announces the thoroughgoing other, the other life. If it is not an end, it is a *stroke of counting* in the profoundest tally of the world; and this tally may signify the gong of passage from the labored sketch to the freedom of a new canvas, or from the apprenticeship in creativity to the exercise of a maturer art.

Putting away the unfinished work of the dated self may then be looked on, if not with less regret, as least with full recognition of the measure of its release from what was irrational. (This is the truth which Plato felt and mistook as a release from the body.) For death would mean sifting away the accidental specifications, destroying manacles, emancipating the self from connections in part stultifying, or maintained by a mechanical momentum rather than by inner vitality, releasing deep loyalties and loves from every blight of habit, and strong purposes from the barnacles of formulae and the conventions of a career destined to decline in fertility. Fertility runs down through a deficiency of otherness. And death, bringing one to the "other of all this," may be the method whereby aging beings, such as minds are, can recover not alone that inner agelessness which belongs to physical energy, but the whole freshness and meaning of that past set of belongings which had begun, unjustly, to forfeit its savor.

The one thing that death would not mean, under these suppositions, is eternal rest.

For continuance can have no sense unless the reflective self is concrete and active, carrying on that questioning which is the identity of its life here and through all possible lives, and through whatever changes of categories. If death means rest and sleep, death is final. There is, we think, too much soul's ease in this conception, and nothing to support it but the weariness of aging muscles, and the decline of values, belonging to that dated self, which *is* weary and shall have peace. For the surviving self, death must be the renewal of that negative wholeness of the subconscious self which is its innocence of limitation. It would mean passage to another effort, with revised direction, in an ampler world.

As a consolation for incompetence and defeat, the concept of another life has no legitimate use: it has every use for the continued will to understand the sense of suffering and thwart. The continued craving for that which is not, that restless anxiety and pain, which lies at the core of our being—that deep-buried burning concern which the pessimist misinterprets as the defeat of our happiness—that is in reality the soul's loyalty to its own goal, its underlying faithfulness to its destiny. It is the best indication that this infinitude of possibility, unfulfilled even in the most fortunate, rests on the underground waters of being as a compass whose direction the currents of reality are to honor. If any selves go on they are selves that suffer; but they are also the lovers of life, not its haters.

VII

WHAT OUGHT TO BE

WE have been speaking of possibilities, not of proofs. If we are right, the common grounds on which survival is excluded as impossible vanish upon examination. The improbabilities are rejected as impertinent. And the idea of another life, though it lends itself neither to verification by us nor to imaginability, is not devoid of meaning.

But herewith the office of analysis is done. Our thoughts are released by these findings. But our eventual judgment will be determined by other things, such as these: *analogy* —analogies and contrast between the rhythm of life and death and other rhythms our course of life is subject to, or analogy with other deaths which are in life, as of childhood or of suppressed selfhood, and the rebirths which succeed them; *attunement*—finding a just balance of judgment in the perpetual tension in ourselves between a sobriety which may be dull and unseeing and a vision which may be visionary; *valuing*—a total sense of the fitness or rightness of one fate or another. All these belong to the domain of intuition, our resultant intuition about the world we inhabit.

I wish now to summon you to such an intuition as the reflections of this hour may afford, and in preparation for that effort to make note of one truth which has less repute than it deserves: the truth that *duration is a dimension of value.*

It is common to suppose that quality alone is important; and that when experience has a satisfactory or noble quality, prolongation adds nothing to its worth. One hears the phrase "mere continuance," and thinks with aversion of a purely animal tenacity of being, willing to spin out through endless time the torpor of a tortoise or the vegetable somnolence of a sequoia. To experience happiness or greatness or intensity or elevation or ecstasy for an instant—that is held to be the goal; and then one may vanish content. And doubtless if the choice were between a long-continued humdrum and a brief flash of flame, it is better to be able to say "I have lived" than to say "I have lasted." But these are not the only alternatives. And for the one who, being gone, is no longer able to look back and say "I have lived," there is no better and no worse.

It is the normal destiny of experience to be prolonged in proportion to its height, not inversely. The best of our experiences are normally long looked-forward-to and long remembered: whether the event itself is brief or extended, its time room is measured by the period of its occupation of consciousness in prospect, experience, and retrospect. Without this natural time dimension we know we have not "done justice" to the event: meanings may be seen instantly, but they are not "realized" (by beings with our time-extended mode of thinking) except with a certain amplitude of the process of pondering. Deprived of their due aftergrowth they fail to attain their proper value.

But if time is a dimension of value, it is not a problem to be settled by introspective questioning or questionnairing whether one does or does not desire to continue his life: life is objectively worth more as a continued than as a closed affair. We instinctively know this to be the case. As the impression prevails that this natural world is the only world, and this life the only life, there arises also a minor point of morals: "Do not waste time thinking about death; live well the time you have, and forget that it ends." For to remember that there is an absolute end does something, in spite of good will, to cut the nerve of present effort. But what sort of realism is this, and what sort of universe, when it becomes a duty not to dwell on the facts? Especially such a fact as the end of individual consciousness, which is pertinent to every undertaking of that individual.

One symptom of this curious unrealism of the realistic bent is a set of fallacies it begets, as it seeks to replace the thought of individual extinction with more hopeful themes.

We are urged to remember that the race goes on, society goes on, institutions go on, and probably "progress": humanity will reach its ideal. The continuance of the social whole may compensate for the loss of the individual. But this is the plausible *fallacy of totalism.* Unless the individual continuance is secure, there is no security for the race. From the point of view of naturalism, the presence on this obscure planet of the conditions suitable to human life or to any life is a rare accident, and in all probability a transitory one: there are many possible events, slight in the scale of cosmic happenings, which would effectively terminate it. It retains its place precariously, at the courtesy of forces it can hardly know nor measure, and which in turn neither know nor care for it. If, then, the individual survives his death in another environment, something of the racial wealth of meaning may be kept when the race is gone. If the individual perishes, the prospect for the race and all its mental treasures is extinction. It is thus the individual who must secure the race, not the race the individual.

We are also urged to remember that new individuals always replace the old, and presumably of a slowly rising mental and moral stature. But no new consciousness can replace the consciousness of the old; for there is a definite value in the continuous climb from zero, and in its remembrance. The meaning of things is increased by the cumulation of the past with which one thinks them: no one knows what an achievement is who does not know the tentatives in which it began. To suppose that new values can stand full-fledged by themselves is one form of the *fallacy of isolation*: new value is relative to the whole of a preceding history. The loss of memories from the world would thus be a clear and irreparable loss of meaning.

But suppose that individuals do not survive, what things in the universe *are* eternal?

Many sorts of thing have been conceived as everlasting —space and time, atoms, the total energy of the world, the sum of energy and mass, the ageless ultimates of physical analysis. Or delivering all particulars over to flux, then ideas and truths and laws of change; for these cannot cease to be themselves nor to be true, whether or not they are known.

Now of all these objects, no one of them knows its own eternity. These ultimate physical units, or the vast world room itself, of the silent, incessant administration of natural law—none of these knows that it is lasting. Nor are the Platonic Ideas aware of their immortality!

But if lastingness is a mark of value, is it not an absurdity of a universe in which the everlasting things are things which do not know and cannot become aware of their post of honor?

And since it is we who have discovered or surmised their perpetuity and thus in our thought have imputed immortality to them, shall we—so liberal of a continuance which things cannot understand—be the ones to perish from the scene?

It is in such rejections of absurdity that the intuitions of mankind most clearly speak—more clearly than in a positive affirmation that immortality must be true.

There are those who affirm their certainty of survival. And for many persons there are occasional moments in which that positive sense of indestructibleness emerges and then subsides. It comes, not as a sporadic emotional exaggeration of the sense of life, but as something seen and clearly judged; as if one had been admitted for an instant to the weighing-places of the powers of the universe, and had perceived that this sort of thing, the self, cannot be destroyed by *that*! It is akin to the immediate awareness of freedom, as the capacity to initiate change from a point just outside the circuit of natural causes; it may be another phase of the same thing. It is, I believe, what Plato meant when he said that there is something in the nature of life which cannot mingle with death. And there are some—I am not among them—who have never doubted that life goes on.

To most of us, I presume, intuitive assurances can go no farther than this: we know that death plows deep, but not to the bottom: it does not break the links and cables of renewal.

But do we not also know that survival *ought to be?* Perhaps it is some false modesty of the soul, some cosmic *mauvaise honte*, which hesitates to press that original *right to endure*, of which we first spoke. This modest trait doubts whether human judgments of what is fit and right would hold for the wider universe; it is governed by a sense of the relativity of the human valuations, especially when one judges one's own case. But such mock meekness —a popular pretense of our time—carries the notion of relativity farther than it is capable of going. For if in the long run our values are to be reversed, then our "great" becomes "small" and our "small" "great"; our "part" becomes "the whole"; we who are puny fragments change places with the universe, and our attempt at supreme self-abnegation turns into the sublimest arrogance. And if our values are not to be reversed, then something of them remains valid. It is impossible to reject what our deepest judgment of fitness asserts; and we may make bold to think that what seems to us irrational cannot in any wider exploration of the world prove to be the truth.

Intuition cannot be wholly wrong. We have reason, however, to be suspicious of a false perspective. We must beware of converting a persuasion that survival must be possible into a conviction that survival is necessary and universal. Survival might conceivably result from an inherent indestructibility; but it might also result from the happy accident that destructive forces pass one by, or from the protection of an outside power or from compliance with a law. Plato would have the soul such a being that no power in the cosmos could either make or unmake it: it is a monad he thought, which can have no beginning, nor ever cease to be even at its own ardent desire. But it seems unlikely that the resources and powers of the individual self are such as to shoulder their way to permanence without reference to the world beyond it. Besides the intuition of continuance, we have also an intuition of dependence—some would say of "absolute dependence": one is as valid as the other. The analogy of human history may be of some aid here; for there is a sort of artificial immortality there provided not by one's own force but by the state. There is no inherent imperishability of any human work, not even of a Shakesperean sonnet: such works endure only so long as ordered human society endures and preserves them; and the state, intending to be undying, lends to human society its own permanence. Human deeds thus borrow their immortality from the state, which traffics in that article; and man makes the state! So perhaps in the cosmic order, there is a thing essentially eternal; and there may be conditions under which the human self participates in its quality.

In my own view, this is the case: survival of death is a possibility but not a necessity of destiny. We have begun this present existence without our prior consent (a mode of entrance inappropriate for a self-sufficient, indestructible atom). Some presumption of a retroactive consent may be seen in the channels of mental heredity, through which the momentum of parental will-to-live might run to the newborn. But being here, we constitute ourselves judges and administrators of the worth of living; and what we come to conceive as fit tends, I believe, to come to pass in each one's personal destiny. If there were a soul in whom living had bred a genuine aversion, through conscious cultivation of a distaste for life— if there were such a soul, I cannot think it doomed against its will to go on. Or, what is more imaginable, if one became determined to deal with this life as a unique and completed whole, coinciding with the career of the body, satisfied to define himself as the rational animal ending in nothing—I can hardly think survival a necessity for such a soul (though I suspect in most who profess this attitude subconscious countercurrents which may eventuate in an agreeable disappointment!). In any event, the quality of the human self, as I conceive it, is not immortality but immortability, the conditional possibility of survival.

What these conditions of survival may be, the world has many surmises, and no one fully knows. They are not written in a book. They are not revealed by any final authority. They are not vested in any person. Still less are they the private perquisite of any society or historic tradition. They are not a set of rules discernible in mystic states or discovered by esoteric discipline. They are not divine codes meant to deflect conduct from its human grooves by setting a great prize for conformity. These represent aberrations of the human hope reaching out for definition, and illustrate the handles which every great hope offers the exploiter.

Neither does any man know fully through self-consciousness what in himself might render him viable beyond death. He does not so much as know what it is that keeps him alive in his present situation. It must be something simple, for it is so natural to live, to think, to be—so little of an effort—so little a possible object of effort. He knows something, at any rate, of what it is not: it is not natural prowess, nor acquired capacities, nor any proud work of the excursive self. If anything can see him through the crisis of death it will be as near to him as breathing, and as elusive as that which now keeps him in being. If there are conditions for survival, they must be as simple as the saying, "As a man thinketh (of himself) in his heart, so is he," and as natural as the passage by growth from one stage of readiness to another. Perhaps our figure of the germinal self may offer an inkling: the process of living this present life *well* might render the fertile soul pregnant with otherness, and unknown to itself gravitant toward a new birth.

This is consonant with flashes of insight which have lighted the race, have been embodied in its saviors, and, treasured in the great traditions, have constituted their valid essence. They indicate that survival may be a matter of the *degree of reality* which the self attains. For the reality of the self is not a fixed quantity: the self is more or less real, more or less a cherisher of illusion, more or less sham and pretense and self-deceit; the deepest law of duty is to put off falsities and achieve what reality we are capable of. And this achievement has doubtless something to do with one's power to love, since it is the nature of love to penetrate through show and artifice to the inner realities of things. One is as real, we said, as what one can create out of oneself; and only the lover knows what to create, and how. The durability of the self, we think, must depend much on the truth of its interpretation of love— itself a riddle deeper than that of the Sphinx, and slaying its tens of thousands for their guilty-false guesses; for love, which as Plato saw is a longing to make immortal, is also in its promise a power to become immortal: "he that loveth aright is born of the immortal One."

And of that outer fact on which survival depends, we can know this, that "substance" and "energy" are not its final names: it is not these which, when a man dies, will receive what entered into him, as a quantum of magnetic dust. For death is not the erasure of life by an entity called Death, nor by an entity called Nature. Death is an encounter of the real with the Real: and the Real, whatever it is, is conscious and living, not inanimate.

Perhaps this is all we need to know of the ways and conditions of survival; but what we chiefly know is that *it ought to be.* For unless there is a way for the continuance of the human self, the world is full of the blunt edges of human meanings, the wreckage of human values, and therefore of the failures of God.

EPILOGUE

THE notion of survival haunts the dark corners of modern consciousness like an uneasy ghost, having no place in the day's business nor in the counsels of state-building sciences. In philosophy, it has the status of an inheritance, finding residual attention as a last chapter, an appendix, a footnote to other matters.

Just on this account, its position as religious dogma is of primary importance; for here a faltering yet vital human concern most needs the considered respect and guidance of racial insight. This responsibility, requiring newly living perspectives as human experience alters its outlooks in other fields, is today largely evaded or mummed by religious institutions, caught timorously in their ancient imagery. This imagery which taken literally is obnoxious to the sounder instincts of mankind they are seemingly reluctant to translate, while rightly unwilling to abandon survival as a total casualty in the path of scientific advance.

In this impasse, philosophic thought, however hesitant, must enter as an interpreter, beginning with a clarification of the meanings of death and of life as they confront one another. With these meanings in mind, we may in due time open the ultimate issue of possibility, in the light of the sciences as well as that of prophet and poet, spokesmen for the intuitions of the race.

PART II

INTERLUDE:
A SYMPOSIUM
ON THE
MEANING OF LIFE

It is not usual to ask people point-blank what they consider the meaning of their own lives or of life in general. Nevertheless, the question is one on which most mature people have meditated at some time or other; for whether or not anyone has put the question into so many words, experience is sure to have put it sooner or later, rudely and silently. It is perhaps the one speculative question on which everybody has a view, based on pertinent evidence; and further, on which all sober views are weighty. For what a man thinks his life means, comes very close to what he thinks he is.

Attack some person, then—someone, if you like, whose life seems to be carried on with a healthy, naïve, unquestioned conviction that it means something—attack him abruptly with the question what he conceives that meaning to be. The chances are that he will be surprised. The chances are also that he will have some sort of significant answer ready, to the equal surprise of the questioner. He will probably profess his answer accidental and inadequate; it will doubtless be so; but it will have in it a fragment of the sense of human existence.

To bring a number of such fragments together may be a useful prelude to a later technical analysis.

I

THE WORTH
OF MERE BEING ALIVE

MOST human beings, we say, meditate on the meaning of life; but few of them drive these meditations to a clear picture of their final aims. One reason for this lies in the fact that the simple going-on of living has an intrinsic satisfaction of its own, which philosophers commonly forget, but which is never far from the surface of common sense. Our questioner may find some answers to the effect that the meaning of life is in being alive!

This is far from being an empty answer. There is a certain pseudo-futurity about the values of living, by which the prophets of flux are systematically taken in— and by which humanity frequently takes itself in until it bethinks itself. Conversation, for example, professes to flow toward some result; but toward what result? Conversation is seldom so much for the sake of developing ideas as for the sake of being with a friend, maintaining active consciousness of his presence. The same is true to some extent of all activity: apart from the ends toward which it aims, and which make its excuse for being, action enhances the direct awareness of being alive which requires no further justification, but which on the contrary goes far to justify the pain of action.

On its lower level, the fact of being conscious is directly enjoyed: an infant requires no "end." And this conscious level is so far held to for its own sake that it resists dropping into a still lower level even for sleep, as if it knew that to be aware of things is intrinsically better than not to be aware of them. This is the mental counterpart of the property sometimes regarded as the primary character of organic life—self-maintenance: perhaps it is the original from which that organic self-maintenance is derived. Wherever the world-process develops a new "emergent," it seems to set at the same time an automatic guard like a notch or ratchet which keeps the new attainment from slipping back. Thus, when mind emerges, it will tend to maintain mentality through simply enjoying mentality.

In the human being, this animal self-enjoyment has become something more, an enjoyment of being intelligent —of judging, thinking, deciding. An infant repeats the name it has learned for no ultimate purpose but for the pure joy of mental action—the mastery of the new word is not the object but an incident of the mental play. For the adult man there is the same kind of pleasure in making an observation; to the logician the observation may be an "induction" or a "deduction"; but to the man himself it may be a quip, a comment, a witticism, a "piece of his mind"—nothing but a sample of his own type of world-awareness.

This immediate sense of worth in living accounts to some extent for the human phenomenon of "idling." The state of mind of the typically "worthless" man is seldom that of a pessimist, nor is it necessarily unintelligent.

The uneconomic man, primitive or other, who drifts and "basks," vaguely interested in the round of nature and in momentary events, with the gossipy consciousness of the pure spectator—this man is no animal. He may be a parasite, a loafer, a porch-rocker, a dowager living on deceased husband's income, any sort of consumer who fails to produce, looked at with semi-envious semi-murderous eyes by the economic intelligence: but at least he is the sociological exaggeration who demonstrates what on the activity theory of worth ought to be impossible, that merely to live may be a sufficient worth.

And he may be much more. He may be, in dumb way, accepting the Universe and his part in it, "glorifying God" and beginning to "enjoy Him forever." The Balinese, according to Geoffrey Gover, carry this capacity for human immediacy to the level of art:

> Here men equal their surroundings. It is not only their comeliness or even their frank enjoyment of life, but also that they make of their life a complete art-integration. . . . And their most moving spectacles . . . are to the Balinese themselves not at all artistic performances but religious rituals in which there is no room for a non-participating audience.

This is the holiday consciousness which civilized man attains perfectly only in exceptional moments. To achieve it more truly he may retreat, with Gauguin or Norman Hall, to Tahiti. But he cannot remain there and retain his sanity; for he cannot become the Tahitian or the Balinese who does not know the world such a modern has left. The goings-on of that modern world, however he may abhor them, continue to infect his retreat, and his sense of worth refers itself to them. When the world is in a stew, he cannot get satisfactory "meaning" in the South Seas, nor in the divinest human immediacy. He feels his joy a

stolen one, and touches in its elemental form the Puritan's
sense of sin. The enjoyment of immediate worth functions
for the normal man as a ground note, entering into every
chord, but seldom acting alone.

Play, which has no age limit, shows the lurking presence of this immediate value sense. It is peculiar to childhood only in the sense that all the activities of children
enjoy the immediate pleasure of action: doing the next
thing always carries meaning enough. The suggestions of
instinct act as starters of action; and life carries the movement of consciousness on from point to point until one
gets a conception of the trend of it. To the less intricate
mind of simple cultures, this play consciousness remains,
and the deed justifies itself in simply being done. The
dead city of Angkor, consisting of lovely monumental and
empty façades, was never built, we are told, for occupation—it was built "to the glory of God." It may be for
a similar reason that the noble medieval architecture of
Asia is allowed to fall into decay: it was the fruit of impulse, which, building monuments to its great, to its dead,
to its gods, was chiefly satisfying itself, and had little
interest beyond the element of worship (free, like play,
from direct purposefulness) involved in the constructing.

The immediate worth of living—not often singled out
for celebration—is thus a fact which we must put at the
base of all reflection on this subject. It may be rather the
subconsciousness of our symposium than any explicit
voice: yet it is pervasively present. This premised, most
people of what we call a modern state tend to find the
meaning of life in some more explicit value. To many, it
lies in something done, achieved, accomplished.

II

WORTH IN DOING
AND IN THINGS DONE

A MAN is likely to identify the meaning of his life with his work. An architect, studying at Beaux Arts, decided that he had but one religion—to understand architecture and to practice it. There was no end to architecture's immensity and depth, there was enough of it to dignify a life.

This has been the experience of many persons entering an occupation which has a tradition into which a million human heads have set each one an idea, until the whole exceeds the capacity of any head. Such a tradition is itself a world of meanings, which one must labor to possess any part of. To perceive meaning is to participate in it: to embody it in work is to possess meaning. The ratio of intake to outgo is not important.

Now work on specific jobs seems at first to locate its meaning in the task to be finished. The operations leading to that end are so much irksome delay and price-paying imposed by the "reluctance of nature." In point of actual experience, this vestibule of travail is all along attended by the awareness in imagination of the object to be gained, and hence the steps up the mountain are not merely so many steps, but so many ingredients of the total satisfaction. Work, imaginatively pursued, becomes as it were, the higher (and prolonged) immediacy of the final objective. Hence work, which seems the reverse of immediacy, tends to resolve itself into an immediacy of more intricate structure.

The more exertion is called out by intensity of opposition—as in battle, or in adventure—the more the experience partakes of the direct tang of being, and justifies itself, at least in retrospect, wholly apart from the end achieved. One who had been in the brief battle of Manila said, "I have lived for at least three minutes." It is the rising of faculty—all faculty—to its height of power in apprehending what is there in the world, what men are, and obstacles; and what wit, strength and speed can do to meet the swift change of the scene. In its dramatic extreme of demand, work becomes once more of the quality of play. It is not important what is done, nor what is thought: what is important is how much being is concentrated in that moment.

Herbert Allen has somewhere remarked about the concentration of war: "you think none of those fancied thoughts about God, home, hereafter; you are too busy": but you live, and the magnet of meaning turns ever after back to that experience as its best example. We require for peace something more than a moral equivalent of war: we need an intensity-equivalent of combat. The development of sportsmanship out of play tends toward an artificial cult of "thrills"—exploration, mountain climbing, big-game hunting, various types of adventure-seeking— as a tribute to the sort of immediate meaning which is normally incident to intense action in "work."

The work of earlier man becomes the play of later man:

openings of the seasons for hunting and fishing, the tasks
of gardening and the taming of animals, the mastering of
the sea, all provide strains that enter into joys; the values
of success are measured by the effort, also by the danger,
of the action. Civilization has no greater triumph than
the full participation of the laborer in the meaning of his
product; it can have no greater failure than the transloca-
tion of the worker's satisfaction from his "work" to his
recreations: the drive for lessening the hours of labor has
been a boon—a necessity of the mechanizing of industrial
processes—but the ideal of the four-day week, moving on
to the three-day week, and so to the terminus, is a calumny
on the spirit of production, and a prophecy of social collapse. A man's work is normally the most tangible
embodiment of his will-to-power, his most immediate testi-
mony to his worth as a man.

III

WORTH IN LOVE AND APPRECIATION

IF achievement were the sole source of the meaning of life, those who for any reason are deprived of achievement, would find their lives *ipso facto* meaningless. Yet there are those who do little work, and who find a sufficiency of meaning for life in the experience of loving and being loved. So long as one has a friend, one can endure to be, though nothing is accomplished beyond the maintenance of that strange mutuality and indirection of consciousness.

It is hard to say what one being adds to the being of another. It is not the simple reflection of one's own mental face, which one might willingly not see even through friendly eyes. It is partly that one can authoritatively confer a sense of worth by loving the other, and what confers this sense cannot be worthless. The existence of a quality in the beloved is not complete in merely existing; it is fulfilled only as it is discovered, admired, proclaimed. The mind which thus perceives and announces beauty seems to fulfill its own being, and also that of the other.

Love makes no absolute insistence that the excellence of the beloved is superior to that of others—it is not interested in comparisons. What it perceives is that the living human being is marvelous. You have shown me the intrinsic loveliness and wonder of life, of body, of hand, of eye, of carriage, of the common operations of thinking, looking, speaking. Love is an admission into the miraculous quality of the commonplace. In thus comprehending the hidden springs of worth in living, the lover first feels in his own life a dignity he had not suspected, and cannot repudiate. What further meaning does he need than this?

The poets are likely to make much of the adequacy of love as a justification for the pain of being. "Love wakes men, once a lifetime each," says Coventry Patmore, and he assumes that it is awakening they need, not any special stuff of experience.

> Love wakes men, once a lifetime each,
> They lift their heavy lids and look,
> And lo, what one bright page can teach,
> They read with joy, then close the book.
>
> And some give thanks, and some blaspheme,
> And some forget, but either way,
> That, and the child's unheeded dream,
> Are all the light of all their day.

But there is a mystery about love, which is seen, in part, in its evanescence. Why is the book shut? And why, if one has known the secret, should that glory and aura of loving be so irrecoverable? Can love be understood?

In analysis, love appears as a perception of qualities, such as can be singly held out for appreciation. Every perceiver of worth is, so far, a Platonic lover. And one will agree that in so far as worth is actually present and being enjoyed, life is in possession of meaning. The amateur in art or science is the nobler epicurean, who through initiation has attained to the joys and sorrows of the connoisseur. If he is faithful to his love, he will say that it is better to have the true and jealous taste, with its attendant suffering, that to be satisfied with vulgarity. Is the meaning of personal love to be stabilized by being refracted into a prism of appreciations? And are these appreciations the essential meaning of life?

It is largely this belief which explains the drift of mankind into whatever offers itself as "higher education." It is the transfigured Platonism of modernity. I ask a woman student why she holds this insatiate desire to be educated, and she replies that she wishes to be made sensitive to values, those that have reality; this, she thinks, is what life means; she requires depth in experience, rather than frequency or intensity, to the extent of her capacity for depth. And her friend, the poet, puts his hoped-for meaning of life in similar language—there are, he says, "certain experience of mankind he does not want to miss." One recalls that Dewey somewhere defines the good in terms of the "multiplication of satisfactions." This perception of the student, that appreciations differ in depth and reality, and that there are certain ones of racial purport which no one ought to "miss," is a kindred analysis of the generalized art of love.

Granting this analysis a sort of collateral significance, it remains true that it has lost the peculiar poignancy of personal love in a plurality of aesthetic enjoyments—for love of a person never yields its reason in terms of qualities intrinsically admirable. The person is more than these qualities, and also less.

For the beloved being is less a spectrum of embodied

perfections than a reaching-out to an unrealized self. The lover loves the beloved's yearning, and his love may be itself a sympathetically awakened aspiration, anxiety, nostalgia. Thus love is a sharing not of possessions but of longings. It is the presence of "soul" to "soul"—the soul being that phase of our being which dreams of the beyond, and lives in what is not at hand. It is an impulse toward comradeship in an endless pilgrimage, now at its beginning. Love raises no doubt as to the sincerity of this aspiration in which it bathes and within which it opens its own wings—a sincerity which will pay the hard price of eternal, self-immolating pursuit.

Yet it lies in the nature of human love to find in this agreement to aspire an immediate good, an attitude having its own intrinsic grace—so sufficient that all that is not present, the objects of aspiration, may be put out of mind. To this extent, love is perpetually tempted to insincerity: it pretends to itself that in having the one who longs, it has all that is longed for. Then when one clasps the beloved, one clasps not the longing searcher, but the present human fact. The immediate union of infinite longing with infinite longing has meant the disappearance of both longings in a spurious attainment: and love, as they say, comes to earth. The stability of love requires a stability of relation to some concrete object beyond the personal context; it is this perception which leads us to look beyond the word "love," whether personal or appreciative for the substance of meaning.

IV

WORTH IN SERVING CAUSES: A UNION OF LOVE AND POWER

THE poet who said that life meant for him some experiences he did not want to miss, added a second objective of familiar sound, "to make the world a little better." This commonplace formula, which may be as far from being negligible as it is from being original, unites the interest in achievement with a form of love, the spirit of universal good will. It is perhaps the most widely celebrated of the meanings of life in a time in which the "welfare of society" or of humanity seems the growing fund from which value flows back on all individual participants.

It is an account of meaning which enables one to project himself beyond himself, and so escape the narrowness of self-interest. It is altruism, but of large dimensions, as of one who perceives some great thing moving in the world, and whose joy is in taking part—if not with assurance, at least with the hope of "contributing."

This source of worth may sink to the amiable banality of the feebly Christianized multitude, who drift into a

sentimental sense of worthiness on the current of repu-
table benevolence. As such it is fit to be spewed from the
mouth of a Nietzsche—or of a John of Patmos. But it is
also capable of sublime heights, and may become the absorbing passion of a stern and noble life.

Sir Wilfred Grenfell found the meaning of his life in a
task in Labrador. He had medical training, and might
have reflected, as did our architect, that the study and
practice of his profession was his religion. But he looked
for something else to do with his power in hand, and was
deflected toward an undertaking on the outskirts of anything one might call "progress." The man who may have
been responsible for this shift would have described his
own ambition as the "saving of individual souls": it was
Dwight L. Moody. But for Grenfell this motive was trans-
formed by a strong community sense. What he has been
doing in Labrador is to take a group of people dropping
off the edge of the human world—exploited, cheated, dis-
eased, devoid of schools and hospitals, slipping out—and
put them back into the world community. It has been a
piece of group surgery: the circulation has been restored.
The native groups have faded out of the scene, too far
gone: the Saxon stock has got its life back.

Grenfell has less to say than we have said of the ultimate motives of his action. He is not interested in "progress" in the usual sense. He finds, we judge, an immediate
satisfaction—assuming the lives of Labradorians worth
while—in wreaking his love for "man" on *them*, and seeing
them get more life. There is an element of the irrational
in it: one chooses this place among many, among these
men, arbitrarily, and finds satisfaction in doing for them.

But what is achieved when such Labradorians are re-
habilitated? Is the result a circle, after all? Lovers of life

take satisfaction in creating more lovers of life. But on these terms, they have not established their own right to a meaning unless each newly established self becomes in turn a creator of further life-lovers; and so the series hangs in suspense for its worth until it shows the quality of endless transmission. This endless fertility, Grenfell and all like him take for granted on the basis of direct intuition, and do not wait for subsequent facts. Their meaning is an immediacy of the second order. The philan-thropic action becomes its own excuse for being, as if, in the Kantian phrase, the good will is good in itself regard-less of results. Or, not quite so subjectively—the good will, producing results, is good in itself without regard to the ultimate history of Labrador. That future is, so to speak, God's responsibility; the word "God" here signifies the factual realization of the intrinsic value of the relation-ship set up, and of the law whereby it tends to reproduce itself.

It is plain, then, that buried in the satisfactions, valid and profound, of such creative good will as that of Gren-fell, there are assumptions about destiny and the frame of things which need a further voice. Altruism, even on the noblest social level, is not a sufficient answer.

V

WORTH IN FULFILLING
A DESTINY

MANY people have a feeling, perhaps a superstition, that they have a specific function to fulfill, which has been assigned to them in the deeper councils of the world. They do not know what that function is. But they are in search of it, kept from a sense of meaninglessness by a conviction that it exists.

It is a version of this view that life has meaning so long as one keeps on growing, that is, continues the progressive realization of capacities assumed innate. But it is something more than this, and less subjective-germ-ripening, when one feels that he is in the hands of an overnecessity which in the course of his world line he could not evade except at the cost of complete futility. The sense of power is to such persons a sense of obligation, and the quest not of inner dimensionality, but of *specific agenda*, as of the thing or things one was meant to do. This sense, I say, may be a superstition. It may mislead into a search for "hints," "indications," "guidance." It does confer an ennobling sense of appointment and of inward relation to the ultimate purpose of things.

Let us designate such persons as the mystics. They are

led on by something they know not what. They are at a
disadvantage in giving an account of it. They may call
it a Grail, or a Beatific Vision, to be sought for not in
something apart from the world but in the strands of
personal activity. The *agendum* is like the military officer's
"mission"; but unlike the officer, the mystic has to find
and decipher his own secret instructions. These strange
souls demand that human action shall bear a stamp of
cosmic appointment, and if they do not perceive that
stamp in the actual present task, they are willing to continue its lead through a long pilgrimage, persistently
expecting the day of recognition: "This is the thing for
which I was born."

If this presupposition were valid, it would evidently
confer adequate meaning upon the life that is working on
its hypothesis. One who is traveling to Mecca to perform
the *Hajj* is not an ordinary traveler. His destination is
present to guide him all the way; at each moment his place
is, not merely a given latitude and longitude, but a certain
distance from Mecca. The possible infinitude of meaning
is thus conserved for the day's motions by this continuous
reference to the awaited discovery. Thus once more meaning enters life not as a goal merely, but as an immediacy—
the highest. The program of the mystic, be it what it may,
is a ritual, and the divine is in it: whatever its labor and
strain, it is the dance of Bali, the quality of eternal play
absorbs its motion and its suffering.

But is it true? Or is it a pleasing myth, the conceit of
spirits repelled by the accidental incidence of accessible
meaning and resolved to extract a more abiding worth at
whatever cost from a silent universe?

VI

THE PARADOXES OF MEANING

A SYMPOSIUM reaches no conclusion. But it may reveal, as running through the various guesses, certain principles which may guide our judgment. It may at the least indicate where the meaning of life is not to be found. Let me attempt to summarize a few such indications.

i. There can be no meaning in life unless there is an immediate meaning.

Meaning cannot lie in postponed satisfaction in some future attainment. However we try to refer meaning to an "end" or "goal," it is the nature of experience to lure it back and weave it in with the quality of the on-going present.

ii. There can be no sufficient meaning of life in immediacy alone.

Meaning is not a taste, nor any sort of purely animal sensitivity; for a human being can take no self-enjoyment in a subhuman form of consciousness. And the human form is actively referring its present to some sort of a beyond which the taster fails to get.

iii. Three sorts of thing put an end to meaning; and when they are applied to the whole of life, they infect the whole of life with meaninglessness. They are:

Death: a termination of consciousness in the unconscious.

Endless sameness, whether in the form of mere prolongation of an unchanging existence, or of repetition, or
of that type of expansion which is sometimes mistaken for
growth, and which consists only of more and more of the
same. This amounts to a form of death, for when life
becomes aware of sameness it tends to become anaesthetic
toward it. Cycles of life which should lead back to the
beginning (as in Nietzsche's *ewige Wiederkunft*) would
be devoid of total meaning; and so also would a spiral
progress which should hover forever over the same point.

Endless deviation: the perpetual abandonment of positions reached. The adoration of novelty destroys meaning
as completely as the adoration of eternal changelessness.

iv. Two sorts of thing put an end to hope:

The end that can never be reached, or that is reached
only at infinity.

The end that is reachable, so that after reaching it
there is nothing more to seek.

From these paradoxes one might draw a pessimist's
conclusion: whatever promises to give life a meaning ends
by destroying it. Mere continuance of what is good turns
it into a torment or a loathing. Life itself runs to a self-
weariness: there is a death from ennui in all tangible joys,
and a revulsion from all intangibles. The presence of this
inner clash of worth-promises made by society, our moral
guides, our own nature, must be clearly faced: Walt
Whitman encounters it, and mutters "Through angers,
losses, ambitions, . . . ennui, *what you are picks it way.*"
This confrontation may help in the way-picking, by indicating the nature of the problem to be solved. If there is
such a meaning, it must unite stability with change; reach-

ableness with eternal elusiveness; immediacy with thought-filled purpose; the care-free enjoyment of the child at play with the anxious concern of the groping self in the service of an undeciphered destiny. This union of opposites life does afford; and through that union a deeper meaning than could be offered by either factor alone. How this may occur, we shall inquire.

PART III

MEANINGS OF LIFE

I

THOUGHT AND SANITY

It is fortunate that neither animals nor men need a theory of the meaning of life in order to begin living. The ordinary processes of living, if they can hardly be said from the first to assert their own value, at least raise no skeptical questions about it. The unreflective, unquestioning assurance that one's existence and doings are worth while is roughly what we mean by sanity. Such sanity, little as it may please the rational animal to observe the fact, is not maintained any more than it is begotten by skill in the arts of reasoning: the meaning of life appears most secure when we are not thinking about it. Nor is this merely an oblique way of saying that we are only driven to think about that meaning when something renders us insecure; for the person who has lost conviction that his life has a meaning can hardly be restored to sanity by reason alone.

We partly understand, then, why it is that when, as today, there is widespread loss of assurance about the meaning of human life, it is not the professional philosopher who is most likely to be drawn into consultation, nor yet the clergyman. It is more likely to be the psychiatrist. In his practice, Dr. C. G. Jung finds this question: What is the meaning of life, or of *my* life, "the most ordinary and frequent of questions." What is the reason for this preference? Assuming the broad distinction that science deals with facts and religion with the meaning or value of facts, it would be natural for this question to be referred to the religious authority; but according to Dr. Jung mental sufferers are less likely to turn in this direction, because "they know too well what the clergyman will say." And as for consulting the philosopher, "they smile at the very thought of the philosopher's answer." [1]

What is it that the clergyman is expected to say, and why is it considered useless?

This matter of the meaning of life has been considered important enough to be set into the catechism, under the caption, "What is the chief end of man?" and the answer is, I believe, "To glorify God and enjoy him forever." Our ancestors would have been surprised to learn that we find any difficulty in these words; some of our contemporaries are equally amazed that our ancestors found them clear. What is it, they ask, to glorify God; and how can it be the chief aim of one being to glorify another? The meaning of human life ought to be stated, they judge, in terms of human interests; otherwise known and accessible values are made subordinate to unknown and inaccessible values —unreasonable, humiliating, obscure!

Perhaps we feign a little more mystification in regard to this formula than we actually suffer. There is in it a certain evident magnificence connecting the human creature straightway with the ultimate center of things; and there is a promise of eternal and sublime absorption in a good which, however elusive to present grasp, is presumably valid, permanent, and final. We know persons who,

[1] Jung, *Modern Man in Search of a Soul,* p. 267.

taking this view of themselves, have achieved not humilia-
tion, but dignity and peace, and—as if the main objective
had been provided for—have kept into old age the savor
of existence and unflagging interest in people and events.
This is pertinent to our question, but it hardly helps us,
if the terms of the faith have gone beyond our reach.
We can say almost as much for the fighting Moslem of
old who had his myth of impending Paradise which gave
him a sense of glory in the very shafts that plowed him
down. Suppose there is no Paradise, no consciousness, no
more of that man at all; he has at least, to the very end,
felt his life worth living, and this may serve as a psychological recommendation of the myth! But like all the
psychologists' prescriptions, the psychologist cannot take
it—for he cannot immerse himself in the myth—and we
are all psychologists today.

We are inclined to think that there is something of
great value in the theological view, if we could get at it;
but for the present we set the formula aside as a problem
rather than as an answer, accepting Dr. Jung's verdict
that the theologian could help the present generation more
if he could translate his ideas into contemporary language.

The philosopher, however, whose business it is to keep
his speech close to the literalities of the scientific temper—
why should he be a helpless adviser?

Partly, I presume, because he is disposed to large generalities, whereas this question as it affects any person is
terribly concrete and near. The philosopher may set up
an ethical definition of absolute good, and find the worth
of human life measured by the degree in which it embodies
or conforms to that end. Or he may, with Hegel, portray
the march of Reason in the world and urge men to par-

ticipate in this universal movement of the Idea. What *he* says is also pertinent. Yet his majestic ideology tends to ride over and beyond the acutely individual pass in which the problem takes human shape, and to reverse its perspective: it is as if to the philosopher nothing were important except the general truth, whereas to the human person nothing were important except the particular.

Partly also because the very attitude of rational inspection and analysis cuts across the momentum of the vital stream in which meaning naturally floats. Meaning, like appetite, *vient en mangeant*. There is much in· the pragmatic advice: act first, seek your justifying flavor afterward.

But is there not some absurdity in proposing action as an answer to the question of life's meaning, when action of itself makes no statements? The pragmatic prescription may be good in special cases, especially for beginners. But if one has acted, and the salt of action has lost its savor, it will not be salted by more activity! If the present age is suffering, as no previous age has suffered, from the disease of meaninglessness, it is certainly not due to a deficiency of action! And while an attitude of reflection, which interrupts action for a moment, has to suffer from its own imperfect embodiment of life, it is but preparing for better action; for action always employs *some* thought. It is not a choice between thought and action; but between action guided by a worse thought and action guided by a better thought. Hence it is impossible that reflection, in its own nature, can be an enemy to meaning.

It is more likely that the malady of meaninglessness is a disease of growth than a disease of thought; and the fact that it is a malady of which only civilized and reflective man is capable is at least semi-creditable to the sufferer.

Primitive man is wholly free from it. Reversion to primitivism is one of the avenues in which modern man has sought relief, on the theory that primitive man must somehow be possessed of the secret. Norman Hall, tired of the mess of war, locates himself in Tahiti as Gauguin and others had done before. But they cannot divest themselves of their reflectiveness; and neither Tahiti nor any other primitive spot has an answer; for how can one possess an answer to a question one has never raised?

The same difficulty is met if we try the kindred cure proposed by Bergson—appeal to intuition as against the intellect. The intellect is always raising problems, says Bergson, which only intuition can answer, though it would never occur to intuition to ask them. But in this case, intuition can neither comprehend the question nor answer it. The point is, that once a doubt has been raised about the worth of living, a critical point of moral evolution has been reached; and there can be no going back into an unquestioning innocence, and no answer except in the terms of the question itself. Hence philosophy is involved, because the asking and answering of this question *is* philosophy.

And whether or not philosophers are consulted, philosophy cannot evade the question. For philosophy is committed to the view that the universe has a meaning—which it is out to find; and that human life, by inclusion, has a meaning also. If its answers have been husks, that is due not to the nature of reason but to bad reasoning.

The alternatives are but two.

Either there is no answer to the question of the worth

of life: Then primitive man, the fool of nature, nose-led by his instinctive drives, which he feels to be full of meaning, is happier solely because he is unsuspecting of Nature's ruse. And we, having become self-conscious, are fated to bear the penalty of disillusionment.

Or else there is an answer: Then primitive man becomes instructive to us in a different way—no longer as an impossible ideal, nor as harboring a profound secret, but as using in his naïve attitudes valid intuitions whose meaning reflection, rendered sadder and honester by its failures, may recognize and interpret in intellectual terms, not without bearing on contemporary problems.

The first alternative—that life has for thoughtful men no total meaning—cannot be dismissed with a word. There is a wisdom in pessimism and in this kindred judgment of the worth void (like that physical vacuum in which the universe was once supposed to float): it is the wisdom of a wider survey.

In its biological frame, life appears as a set of instinct activities, the conclusion of one the beginning of the next, forming a life cycle. But a cycle implies that the terminus of one life is the beginning of another: hence a succession of life cycles which are the same forever. From the scientific point of view, this mode of conceiving things is a triumph; for science is the discernment of series in the confused changes of the world. But series involve repetition, and repetition the banishment of meaning. Hence our theoretical triumph begets a new and better-grounded pessimism, not the pessimism of complaint, but the pessimism of emptiness.

This result will be much before us during our argument. It seems clear, however, that there can be no such thing as a demonstration of the meaninglessness of life; one can

only report that one has not so far found a meaning, and
it is always possible that the fault is in the direction of
one's search—one has been trying to draw water from
empty wells.

The second alternative I take to be the true one: there
is a meaning; primitive intuition grasps it dimly; it is
capable of rational expression, with an increase of force,
not a loss of it. We shall try to find such an expression.

When philosophy in search of "substance" betakes itself to "animal faith," it is celebrating its most signal
failure. When in search of meaning it betakes itself to
"animal drives" it parades its shame as if it were an accomplishment. Reversion to simplicity and . vitality we
must have; but not as a new version of the ancient irra-
tionalism, a new divorce such as Bergson proposes between
vitality and intelligence. What we require is the opposite
of this—a remarriage between vitality and intelligence,
which have been living too much apart in attempted independence and mutual criticism.

With this conviction, I shall invite you to consider
certain logical discriminations which I find useful in dealing with the notion of meaning.

II

LOGICAL PRELIMINARIES

We cannot get far in our inquiry here (and this is true of a good deal of contemporary philosophy) without some general notions about "meaning."

Meaning is not a single sort of thing: it is at least two-fold, that is, we have to look for it in at least two directions. The meaning of a generality has to be looked for in the particulars which it covers. The meaning of a particular has commonly to be looked for in a generality.

If, for example, we are asked the meaning of the very general term "beauty," there is little satisfaction in trying to define it in terms of other general ideas, such as "value." But we get some light on it when we are told that it means a quality such as one finds in this and this and this beautiful thing. The general means these particulars. On the other hand, if we are asked the meaning of a particular, we shall frequently find that it has a meaning because it exemplifies some general rule or class. This red spot on the skin means nothing to you and me; to the physician's eye it means scarlet fever. This bird's flight is an instance of migration; it means the approach of summer. The position of this star on the photographic

110

plate is a mere fact to the lay eye: to the astrophysicist it means corroboration of a theory that light is deflected by gravity. And as a rule, the power of an intellect can be roughly measured by the amount of general significance which a given particular may carry.

It is clear that a theory which lights on the first of these two directions of meaning—whereby the general means the particular, as logical positivism inclines to do —and calls this the meaning of meaning, is dealing with a half-truth as if it were the whole. A satisfactory theory must recognize both directions of meaning, and show how they are connected; failing to do this, it merely spins on its heels among old dilemmas.

This is one instance of a general principle in philosophy which I shall call *the principle of duality* (in analogy with the correspondence principle in projective geometry). We shall not try here to make a formal principle of it, but merely use it as a guide to judgment, suggesting that certain relations between ultimate categories can be read in either direction with equal validity.

Thus, in regard to the meaning of life—which is here not a definitional meaning but a value meaning. In one direction, life finds its meaning in spots of valuable experience, particular goods—pleasures, successes, and the like. This is the most palpable meaning of life. Each particular good suffuses the path that leads up to it with meaning. If I am a hunter, the meaning of what I am now doing is the kill at the end of the hunt, or the feast beyond the kill, or the pride and glory in my prowess which may last well beyond the feast. Thus, the bundle of one's particular hopes provides meanings for the total complex of all those activities that lead toward them, even if they never arrive. But true meaning is found in the moments that do arrive, in spots of enjoyed experience; and all other meanings are subsidiary and derivative.

On the other hand, one may reasonably inquire further, what do these spotwise enjoyments mean, singly or in sum? This is the baffling question, and at first sight somewhat perverse: for if labor, pain, delay, all mean the enjoyment in which they hope to terminate, why then turn on this enjoyment and suggest that it mean something else? Enjoyments mean themselves and that is the end of it. There is a logical twist in asking for the meaning of "life as a whole": life contains meanings—it does not have a meaning of its own! Yet it is precisely this which the inquiry for the meaning of life usually has in mind. And it looks for its answer, not toward more of these spots, but in the opposite direction, toward some relation of individual human life to a larger totality.

In the one direction, meaning ascends from the parts to the whole: life has meaning if it contains a goodly number of these satisfactory spots—their worth colors the frame in which they are set. In the other direction, meaning descends from the whole to the parts: human life has a meaning if (and only if) there is a total meaning in the world in which it can participate.

There is a traditional hostility between these two views; men have been called upon to choose between them. Pleasure, for example, has been under common condemnation in philosophy, chiefly because it is a spotwise good, and therefore ephemeral: all genuine meaning, it has been said, derives from the whole—be it the evolution of the race, or the realization of ideals, or the purposes of God. But the empirically-minded man calls attention very justly to the vagueness of these totalities; and further to one striking phenomenon—the apparent evanescence of meaning as one passes from smaller to larger totalities in one's own life. It is easy to tell the meaning of what one is doing today in terms of what one expects tomorrow: but the meaning of this year's activities in terms of the longer purposes of life is more difficult to say! And if one persists in asking what the meaning of these longer plans may be in the total purpose of life—one gasps for an answer. The bride-to-be works on her trousseau because she plans to marry; if you ask her why she marries, she may think you a fool, but may deign to reply that she hopes to have a family and care for them. If you then further ask why she plans to have a family and care for them, she is probably annoyed, chiefly because she has nothing to say. The larger meanings are evanescent. The verifiable source of meaning is the particular.

Now the principle of duality requires that both modes of meaning be true. Pleasure is important. I am prepared to say, as against the philosophic tradition, that pleasure is a necessary condition of the meaning of life. There is a soundness in the common unreflective sense according to which life means the next meal, the next struggle, the next success, and in retrospect, the algebraic sum of all such spots, with a tendency to forget or minimize the negative values. The fisherman has no problem of the meaning of life so long as he is intent on what may happen the next minute. And it is no derogation of this attitude to say that it is the animal attitude: the animal meaning is a part of the meaning of life.

Only, it is not the whole; and the rest of it is not in the same direction! That is the source of the difficulty. The meaning which lies in particular goods provides a plain and obvious theory! All the utilitarians and pragmatists can come to nest in its ample branches. It excludes the other view, not by refuting it, but by displacing it. Nevertheless, it is also true that meaning descends from the whole to the parts.

And the disease of meaninglessness which infects our time is due, I believe, chiefly to the fact that since this second aspect of meaning has not been attended to, human life has been set, through the normal advances of the sciences, into a series of total frames which are essentially meaningless—for it is not the business of science to deal with meanings—and this inadvertency of the age has eaten away the foundations of its structure of meanings. A meaningless whole implies a meaningless part.

We have set human life into an astronomical picture, which by definition contains no meaning. We have psychologized ourselves as things of physical nature—therefore meaningless. We have biologized ourselves as products of natural drives, which result in life cycles—likewise meaningless. We have sociologized ourselves into a humanism of mutual aid, in arriving at biological ends, for which psychology can give us the behavior patterns, which is part of the astronomical scene, which is meaningless. All this is the result of our most exalted intellectual achievement, our scientific reason, accepted as the datum of philosophy.

We are in the position of the patient who arrived near midnight at the door of the Berlin Psychopathic Institute, and having awakened the staff, demanded admission on the ground that he was out of his mind: "*Ich bin verrückt*," he said. This was irregular, for patients out of their minds are not supposed to admit it, and hence the rules required certificates of physicians. But since this patient was confessing his deficiency, the authorities in that emergency saw no reason why the routine should be insisted on: he was admitted, and the subsequent examination showed that his diagnosis of his own condition was correct. But the matter became an embarrassing legal issue, turning on the point that since he had made a true diagnosis, he must in this capacity, have been sane at the moment of admission. The court could deal with the sane and also with the insane; but not with an individual who was both at the same time. Yet this seems to be our own plight, for in the perfection of our sanity, we have soberly adjudged ourselves as a race devoid of meaning. No wonder we patronize the psychoanalysts.

It may be well to look at this situation somewhat more closely, and then inquire whether there are omitted elements in that total scene.

III

SCIENCE AND IMAGINATION

SCIENCE is not in general responsible for the use which men make of its results, whether these users are technicians or thinkers. Science is concerned with facts, not with the value-meaning of these facts. As a body of truth, science stands as one great and indubitable moral achievement of our time. If men misinterpret it, that is their responsibility, not the scientist's.

There is, however, one science of which this cannot be said with the same freedom, namely, psychology. The human mind is a pursuer of meanings and values; a science of the mind becomes, therefore, an inquiry into the entertainment of meaning. And the trend of this science has encouraged the public, and college administrations in America and Germany, to believe that it has light to throw on this theme.

It is therefore obligatory upon us to note that in proportion as psychology succeeds in its ambition to become a natural science, just in that proportion it becomes empty-handed in respect to meanings.[1] For the ideal of

[1] In practice, the science of psychology is pulled in two directions; toward naturalism, perhaps in the form of behaviorism, which is one clear ideal, and toward a purposive description with introspective data. I am here speaking of the pure instances of the first trend.

psychology as a natural science is to reduce the phenomena of the mind to patterns of behavior, which are in the last analysis events in the general history of energy. The entity called "consciousness" may be there, but it is not to intrude into the picture as an explanatory factor. Nothing that happens happens because of consciousness and its desires; it happens because the pertinent law of brain physiology requires this outcome. And since "law" is not aware of what it does, and since all meaning is meaning *for consciousness,* meaning is eliminated from the scientific picture. Thus a natural-science psychology is, by necessity of its method, a description of the meaningful in terms of the meaningless.

Now the methods and working assumptions of psychology are just as legitimate as those of any other science. They are to some extent forced upon it by the nature of its attempt to observe and measure the mind, which is neither directly observable by an outsider nor measurable. It is driven to substitute for the mind the brain, or the organism in its relations to its environment—which *can be* observed and measured. For many purposes these substitutions are valid; and an important body of truth arises from them. It is perhaps too much to expect the psychologist as a human being to remind his public at every turn (or his students, or himself) that his results, as a picture of the human mind, have just one grave defect, adopted with the working hypotheses, namely, that they have no *meaning* at all! But since meaning is our present interest, we have to insist, somewhat ungraciously, on this circumstance. A naturalistic psychology, once taken as the truth about human nature, would become a guide to national mental and moral bankruptcy, not to social control.

The value of the psychologist's results is that they explain our errors—why we *mis*behave. Their defect is that they can never explain why we go right. For the criminal or the neurotic patient, it is a vast comfort to learn that what he has done is the result of certain mechanisms, and can be dealt with, like any other fact of nature, medically. He resorts to the psychoanalyst in preference to the moral philosopher or the priest, largely because he prefers to regard his deviations as natural phenomena, rather than as products of his will. But for the *restoration* of either the neurotic or the criminal, he must be brought back, somehow, into the world of meanings, in which his behavior is subject to standards. Otherwise he is worse off than he was before—as many are—because he has been reduced in his own eyes to an automaton, whose whole existence is devoid of sense.

As applied psychology comes to a clear consciousness of its position, it recognizes this fact. Clearheaded and candid psychiatrists and psychoanalysts, like Dr. Jung, or recently Dr. Link in our own country, feel bound to announce it, much to the distress of some of their fellow practitioners. Jung remarks that all of his patients above thirty-five—and that means most of them—are suffering, at bottom, from this one cause: Their life has no meaning to them. (He also says that they are all educated people; he does not put these remarks together, but they belong together.) And then he adds that as a psychotherapist he does not know what to tell them, nor does any psychotherapist as such! They have come to him because they have heard of the "subconscious" which, as a mysterious realm secure from the deadening analyses of our sophisticated minds, may have healing in it as well as disease. "It must be a relief to every serious-minded person," says honest Dr. Jung, "to hear that the psychotherapist also does not know what to say." [2]

But Dr. Jung knows the *sort of thing* that is needed. The patient must acquire a meaning for his life. And if the psychoanalyst does not know the true meaning, and if the patients for the most part get nothing from religion, the best the physician can do is to bring imagination into play. Hence Jung talks about the "healing fiction"—for after all, an imagined meaning is still a meaning; he finds that the methods of Freud and Adler are deficient because they ascribe "too little value to the fictional and imaginative processes."

Now it is of great interest to note that Professor John Dewey comes to essentially the same conclusion, namely, that the meaning of life is not to be reached through the sciences, but rather by way of the imagination—a conclusion which seems to me in various ways a welcome departure from positions with which he has been supposedly identified.

The genius of the instrumental philosophy I take to be this: that ideas mean what they lead us to—the general idea serves as an instrument to guide action to some particular experience in which it is verified. The general means the particular. But in the great little book of Dewey's on *A Common Faith*, meaning runs the other way; particular experiences appear as *instrumental to ideas*. The meaning of life is found in serving ideal ends, that is to say, in attempting to embody them in practice. To find one's life integrated, that is to say, wholehearted and therefore significant, one must reach the point, says Dewey, where certain ideals present to imagination domi-

[2] Jung, C. G., *Modern Man in Search of a Soul*, p. 267.

nate conduct. Let us look somewhat closely at the reasoning which leads to this conclusion. Its course, as I read it, is as follows:

Ideal ends are suggested by experience—largely by the imperfections of experience which strike out in our minds notions of something better. In this form the ideals do not dominate; they are scattered, occasional, various, they must first be brought into a unity by imagination. They must also be conceived as possible of realization in the universe (which, as Dewey holds, is itself an imagined, not a given totality). Then this projected picture must be regarded as having intrinsic authority over our allegiance. Only in this way can our personal selves be integrated; for the self, also, is not a unity given in experience —the only unity it can possibly have or get is a unity of aim—and it cannot by dead resolve unify itself. There must be some object so intrinsically good that one is, as it were, drawn by it into a "surrender": one is vanquished by the inherent claim of an ideal value. The ordinary, empirical self is not in fact integrated, and in this situation has no total meaning: its unity must come to it from outside, as "an influx from sources beyond purpose." It has, in short, to be unified *by an obligation*; that is, by a conviction "that some end should be supreme over conduct." This surrender has something of the nature of an act of faith because, while the ideals are not alien to the universe which instigates them in us, there is no guaranty that they are to be successfully actualized: "The outcome is not with us." *The ideal may never have a pragmatic verification;* yet the whole possibility of stable and unified living depends on the human capacity to give one's self whole-heartedly to its service.

Now this notion of a surrender to an ideal claim, and,

as Dewey emphasizes, of *stability* through all sorts of vicissitudes because of that single-mindedness (an attitude from which experimentalism seems to have vanished) can only mean that the spotwise values have ceased to be the significant elements in the meaning of life. The part is now to get its meaning from the whole. And that whole is to be presented to us in imagination.

What has brought Dewey to this radically noninstrumental view of things? Nothing but the sterilities inherent in physical naturalism, as the race works out its logic. If the world is indifferent, man is alone with his values; there is nothing for him to do but set up his habitation, defiantly if you please, but at any rate with that will to make the best of things whose true essence is isolation and despair. "The ties binding man to nature that poets have always celebrated" are not appropriate in such a world, and no "natural piety" could be in order. But if human life is to rest seriously, as Dewey urges, on the connection with the environing world "in the way of both dependence and support," we shall have to pass beyond poetry, fiction, or other modes of imagination to the objective facts of that relationship.

If Dewey declines to take this step into metaphysics, it is no doubt because he would then come into dangerous proximity with supernaturalism, which he rejects even more decisively than physicalism. He therefore proposes to depend, for the meaning of life, on the half-world of the imagination.

One wonders, then, whether Dewey's effort to provide life a meaning, like that of Jung, is not *circular*. One has to be integrated by surrender to an outside value; but the self must first of all, in imagination, constitute that outside value, and lend the incommunicative environing world the character of a universe. Can human allegiance be compelled by an object which it has done so much to make? Can the needed "surrender" to a God of one's own conscious construction be genuinely executed?

IV

THE EXPERIMENT
OF WESTERN CIVILIZATION

DEWEY and Jung agree on the valid judgment that the world of spotwise satisfactions lends life no total meaning. Both see that the value of the parts must come from the whole, and that the total pictures revealed by our sciences, so far as they build them, have no meaning to offer from their own resources, and that we have no right to expect it.

Both appeal to the ideal-building imagination to supply this deficiency of science. Now ideals may be imaginary constructions; they can be conceived as unified by imagination. But they may also be regarded as having an objective validity of their own. Plato inclined to set these ideals off in an eternal world by themselves, more real than the world about us; contemporary realism has some leanings toward recognizing their independence, if not their priority. But this detached world, though it does not suffer from being a product of our own fancy, has a similar weakness in its reference to our human affairs. It "subsists" but it does no work. It is just this defect which led to the pragmatic philosophy in the first place, according to which ideals are *not* independent realities to be contemplated, but practical possibilities to be realized. They are not eternal abstractions—there are no possibilities for us except the possibilities we think of. Now when Dewey wants to give them some sort of footing in nature, he is naturally embarrassed. For to regard nature as actually concerned about them would be to turn it into supernature. He therefore leaves their status problematic.

One suspects that Dewey, in accordance with his principles, would like to submit this crucial matter to *experiment*. Fortunately, the experiment has already been performed. It is nothing less than the entire history of Western civilization. One has, of course, to interpret this history. I offer the following unconventional reading of it as a contribution to experimental philosophy.

The history of Europe begins in a period of despair with regard to the spotwise values of life—just such a view as our present age is reaching. There was a spirit of alienation from the biological and social staples of life, arising from a plenitude of experience, and expressing that experience in a variety of ways. Wise men had always warned the race against making too much of pleasure, because indulgence was likely to bring pain. This warning has never been very impressive to impulsive mankind. Wiser men had issued the same warning on another ground, namely, that indulgence is likely to bring shame, which is a very different consideration. Physical greed, for example, was seen to be incompatible with dignity. One could not become the astute diplomat of Ptah Hotep or the princely man of Confucius without keeping a rein on appetite.

Eventually, with more radical analysis, desire itself is

declared the enemy, since it necessarily involves men in suffering. The outlook of Buddhism reflects the widespread judgment of the Orient that the biological lure is deceptive—a nest of false promises, leading only deeper into misery, strengthening thirst in the process of slaking it, fastening the chains that attach one to existence at the moment one thinks one is breaking them. Civilized men had become suspicious of spotwise satisfaction, and, since desire remained, set up *weaning disciplines*, to rid themselves of its illusory spell. The Yoga, the practices of Zen, the negative path of the mystics, are all built on this revulsion against the direct pull of natural value.

Now it is noteworthy that while these weaning disciplines in India and the Far East were motivated by a desire to escape from suffering even at the cost of escaping from existence itself, the two great disciplines which turned westward had very different motives. Neither Stoicism nor Christianity were possessed to escape suffering. They were both preoccupied with the *quality of the person*, so much so as to render them relatively anaesthetic to pleasures and pains. The Stoics wanted inner freedom and self-control—that proud human invulnerability was the possession which made life worth living—and to gain it the more material desires had to be taught their place. The Christians wanted to escape from sin, in order to be fit for another world, and in order to gain this concrete good which was imaginatively felt as almost present, they were not alone already half alienated from the things "after which the Gentiles seek," holding this world in contempt, but were often actually avid for suffering— that persecution and martyrdom which their Master had already held out to them as a reward, and called them blessed when they had it!

What we have, then, in both Stoicism and Christianity is an *experiment in detachment* (detachment from all spotwise goods in the interest of some total good involving self-integration), an experiment carried out heroically by numerous individuals, and transmitted in spirit to the formative period of Europe.

How did this experiment in detachment work? It was, on its literal terms, a failure.

It became clear to the European mind that it is impossible for man to reject the biological and social goods and retain a worth in life. This whole period was a sort of nightmare of otherworldliness from which we are only now recovering.

Upon the *fact* of this failure, mankind is now pretty well agreed; the word "otherworldliness" has become one of the bad words of our vocabulary. When Marx and Bakunin draw up an indictment of religion, it is this that rivets their eye. The weaning is too well done. But we have still to agree on the *cause and the extent of the failure*. Let us look briefly at a phase of history which has never been written, but which is deeper than the history of ideas, namely, the history of feeling—the ruling feeling of schools and epochs.

Stoicism was an aspiration toward unmovedness based on a fear of emotion; it was "imperturbability" based upon a persistent and fundamental perturbation—fear of being perturbed. Stoicism could not last because it was inwardly inconsistent, but also because it was, for each individual, *solitary*—intolerably solitary.

The self-controlled, self-respecting self, proud of its equanimity, free from fear, inflexible in its judgments of

value, enjoying instant by instant the rulership of its own
"ruling faculty"—this self must also be free from any
attachments whose severance could disturb its peace. Life
has to go on; but it moves by rule and relationship, not
by impulse. But a life afraid of its own impulses is something less than life, and something less than free.

Hence we find the Stoics—great, reserved, detached,
lonely, heroic—breaking out of their inward prisons and
seeking an ideal companionship with Destiny, or with
Zeus, if not with mortals. "Lead me, O Zeus, and thou,
O Destiny!" Stoicism veers on one side toward altruism
and on another toward the mysticism which is a flight of
the alone to the Alone!

But this was only to win a certain divine or moral support in detachment, not to achieve any genuine reconciliation with this human sphere of accidental fortune and
injustice. Stoicism could not attach itself, and as a movement, though not as a mighty influence, it perished.

Christian detachment survived longer—partly, I suspect, because it was inconsistent in another way.

Its altruism was, to be sure, a mutual moral support in
otherworldliness; but there was a strange element of *un-
balance* in it. One was to give cups of cold water to others
while regarding these cups of no worth for one's self. The
beneficiary had to be willing to receive what the giver
acquired merit by renouncing. The Christian refused on
principle to fight for his own earthly concerns, but the
earthly welfare of others was worth fighting for; and so
Christianity, with the aid of the Stoics (though with a
pugnacity and persistence which Stoicism never showed)
begot a great system of civil rights—surely a strange
brooding in a camp of world-forsakers!

When the great ages of detachment were over and Humanism began to speak once more for the value of mundane things, Christianity found itself already *half on the side of revolt*. The scientific spirit of the sixteenth and seventeenth centuries was in one sense a reversal of an early-Christian contempt for the wisdom of this world, but in another sense it was a child of this same detachment. For what was the empirical attitude toward nature except a new application of altruism? The scientist must lose his life of *a priori* prejudices in order to save it in the mastery of nature.

Then what has this experiment in detachment shown? That detachment is fallacious and futile and morbid? This is the usual inference. But it is a shollow inference. Such an inference puts us back into the world of spotwise satisfaction—as if *nothing had been learned*. It is futile to go back to that position of mere positive natural chance-taking with the satisfactions of instinctive nature. The despair out of which this stupendous otherworldliness grew was itself an experimental refutation of the sufficiency of the attached life! And if the enthusiasm of the early period of detachment had shown nothing else, it was something for humanity to discover that the moral concern for the quality of the self may become so absorbing as to eliminate or even to invert the natural attitude toward suffering. The attitude of detachment has entered human life to stay.

But it must stay *in company with the attitude of attachment*. The true result of this Western experiment, as I read it, is that detachment and attachment somehow belong together. For there is no worth in living apart from a wholehearted interest in action; and no man can act wholehearted in a world whose values and reality he must hold in constant suspicion or denial. It is the *principle of duality* that is affirmed by this experiment. But it also shows something of the way in which these two opposing directions of meaning belong together. For we observe that it is *only the detached self that is capable of effective attachment.*

If we think simply of spotwise enjoyment, it is not the glutton who most savors the food. To enjoy, one has to be free; so that only he can wholly enjoy to whom enjoyment is no necessity! Similarly, only he is fit for any activity, function, trust, or friendship to whom that good is not the absolute and indispensable good. The best liver is like the true sportsman who treats every game as if it were the sole aim of life, and yet, when it is finished, is not made or unmade by success or failure. The detachment must be genuine in order to be successful.

And if it is genuine, it results not alone in a healthy appetite for the spotwise things, but in *fertility*—inventiveness in those goods which characterize civilization. The enthusiasm with which the methods of science were worked out and the laws of nature conceived and verified was a direct consequence of that long prior restraint. And no mentality which has not acquired a similar power of self-forgetfulness can hope for continued achievement in natural science.

Thus, without intending it, Stoicism and Christianity bred in Europe a race of men capable to a degree unexampled in history of dealing with empirical conditions— capable enjoyers, efficient organizers, able rulers, pertinent and consecutive thinkers, developers of technique, creators of literature and art. It is a blind philosophy of history which supposes that these great traits are products of race, or climate, or economic methods, or reaction against superstition. It was their discipline in detachment which gave them this empirical power!

The psychological conditions of that extraordinary fertility have been the theme of much speculation on the part of historians and philosophers. There can be no insight into it so long as one regards the phenomenon of the Renaissance merely as a humanistic revolt. At least this must be clear: that *detachment had here entered into an auspicious cooperation with attachment*. And our problem is largely what can be meant by *such a normal and genuine detachment* as neither Stoicism nor early Christianity truly defined.

V

HOW ATTACHMENT REQUIRES DETACHMENT

THE CONCEPTION OF GOD

To say that there is such a thing as a normal detachment from human goods is either to say that these goods are of relatively little value and our interest in them ought somehow to be mitigated, or else, without detracting from their value, to say that there is a normal indirectness in the pursuit of them.

We are prepared by what has preceded to reject the first alternative, if not to adopt the second. A detachment which depends on the disparagement of "worldly" or "human" values is unsound, just as any pure otherworldliness is unsound. But why, if human values are valuable, should there be any "normal indirectness"—since an end is, by definition, an object to be aimed at; and there seems to be no virtue in approaching a goal by retreating from it, or in beating a tack to reach it?

a) *The illusion of local value*

The answer lies in the fact that the several goods we seek are not isolated and circumscribable atoms of value.

They are good, but their goodness is not located purely in themselves, any more than the value of a banknote is located in itself as a tangible paper document. The illusion of local value is like the illusion of local weight: the weight of a body appears to be inherent in it—where else should it be? Yet all of this weight could be destroyed without scratching its surface, if we could but destroy all the surrounding bodies. Now consider a value-quality such as the goodness of food; suppose it to be located in the foodstuffs: then it would be no function of our variable appetites, and no matter how much we may have consumed, the food would still retain its same "goodness." But since, in fact, this goodness is clearly relative, among other things, to the health, hunger and habits of the organism, we cannot locate the goodness in the foodstuff.

b) *The general principle of relativity in regard to values*

There is, in fact, a general principle of relativity in regard to value. This principle implies two things:

First, that all goodness is goodness for a self. Whence it follows that a lively and sensitive condition of the self is a prerequisite for any enjoyment whatever; and instead of driving head-on to enjoy, it is occasionally necessary to resensitize the self which is to do the enjoying.

Second, that any particular good is, and is felt to be, a case of a total right relation between the enjoyer and his world. (We are most aware of this in the negative instances in which some outlying and apparently irrelevant uneasiness interferes with such robust and well-localized pleasures as food and sleep.) To enjoy "a good" is always a special way of enjoying "the good." Hence conscious attention to this total rightness may be a necessary precondition for appreciating any specific item of goodness.

Thus what we describe as "a normal detachment" is the natural consequence of seeing more truly than usual what and where goodness is—getting rid of the illusions of its corporeal location and of its independence. A normal detachment is one which looks away from particular goods to the sources from which these goods derive their worth—not to remain with face averted from the "earthly" object, but to return thereto with new zest.

In this very simple statement we have the formal explanation of the universally recognized paradox according to which the direct pursuit of happiness or pleasure proves self-defeating. This self-defeating pursuit is not accurately called a pursuit of pleasure: it is a pursuit of pleasure-in-specific-objects, and it is self-defeating because it falsely locates the value in those objects; it fails to recognize the relativity of what is relative, and the dependency of what depends on something else. There is a lack of objective truth in its definition of its end.

c) *Concrete objectivity*

But what are these "sources of value" to which we must look? Are we being reminded once more of Plato's "absolute good," of which all earthly goods are feeble replicas, and which it is the soul's ambition to contemplate in its purity?

So far as this means that there is a unity in all experiences of goodness, and that it is a condition of health to remind ourselves of this unity, without which we could only be distracted selves, trying to scramble together for our lives a favorable aggregate of disparate satisfactions —Yes! The integration of self depends on the integration of its values.

So far as it means that the world of ideal value in its

unity is a world apart and self-sufficient (as the partial values are not)—No! There is no such world—not even for imagination. If our relief from "this world" can only come by contemplating such ideals as we ourselves can grasp and unify, such principles of improvement as we ourselves have conceived, we are back again in the region in which Dewey, Plato, and Dr. Jung are agreed—the region of the ideal as an abstract object.

Such ideal, an invented notion of what might be or ought to be, an instrument in remodelling experience, has a limited power to claim conviction and service, as well as a limited power to restore the jaded and critical appreciation. It cannot sufficiently detach us from What Is. For What Is, whatever its defects, has shown the vast validity of having come to be: it has reality in its quiver. And further, it is no mere passive receiver of criticism; it criticizes my ideal in turn, and improves it.

It is true that the ideal remains apart from the facts. Every effort to appreciate the facts of experience is saddening, and leads to a return to the ideal as escape and refreshment: art and the perfect realm of number may provide a partial release for "the free man's worship." So too, every effort to embody the ideal is saddening: the ideal stands beyond, with its persistent invitation and demand, holding us subject to it by its own beauty. But it does not stand unchanged! For the effort to embody is also instructive to the ideal itself. The means which we find necessary in order to give our ideas historical effect are never mere "resistances": they contribute to our understanding of what the idea means. The house that is built is less than the house that was dreamed, but it is also much more.

This implies that the ideal is no mere invention of my

own, but in part a discovery. It is in the concrete world, that very world which I am criticizing and detaching myself from. It is there in two senses; first, as partially embodied. This is what Hegel sees: the real element in the flux of history is the rational or ideal part, and the ideal which has shown even the partial merit of coming into existence is a truer ideal than the separate and aloof world of abstract perfection. But beyond this, secondly, the ideal is concretely present as a *tension* in these very things, as if they were at war with themselves, dissatisfied with themselves.

The philosophy of immanence (pantheism, monism, objective idealism, humanism) lights on half of this truth: the absolute is within the world; all things partake of the divine nature. But this philosophy fails to note that the absolute is there also as an ingredient of strain and ferment: the divine nature is at odds with the very particular it inhabits; the essence of the good is dissatisfied with its actual garb and struggles beyond its integument. In criticizing it we are (to some degree) reporting its own self-criticism. In observing a living thing we perceive both what it is and what it aims at, beyond what it is. The ideals we conceive for a thing are likely to be well-founded when they correspond with a tension and conflict within the thing's own nature.

So far as this is true, both of part-things and of the world as a whole, the human product of ideals ceases to be a mere subjective localism in the universe, supported chiefly by private resolve and sentiment as the free man's courageous but also defiant and desperate worship: it becomes an attempt to decipher the inward driving and straining force, the in-tension of things. The ideals cease to be merely ours; they acquire concrete objectivity. To them, as ideal objects, is thus added a *subject*, a self who entertains them: the world knows what it is doing: the locus of what we call "reality" shifts from the particular facts toward this concrete entity, the process of the world as *an intended labor*. Thus in contemplating "the good" we contemplate "the real" as well. Whether or not this is the "supernaturalism" which Dewey dreads may be a matter of terminology; it is, I believe, what he ought to mean. At any rate, the integration of the self, and therewith the vigor of normal human attachment, can be had on no other terms. Our normal detachment is first of all our effort to discern this concretely objective "will of the world," the God who is critic and alterer and not alone the conservative substance at the center of the world.

THE CONTINUANCE OF LIFE

This problem of a "normal detachment," we have said, requires for its solution first of all the recognition of objective reality in an ideal factor in events. This ideal factor shows itself first in the self-enjoyment by the world of its own actualized goodness as its "real" element. It shows itself also as an objective struggle away from what things are toward what they might be. Because of this objective factor, man is not alone in his grasp and support of "the good."

But the law of detachment has another aspect of which we shall gain a clearer view if we consider more closely how any particular spot-wise good is related to its context.

d) *The law of empirical otherness*

It is a psychological commonplace that we know things in part through what they are not. If every colored thing were green, the epithet "green" would lose all the significance it now has by being "not red," "not yellow," "not blue." There might still be a theory of color; but this theory would coalesce with the theory of green, and one or other word would be superfluous, except for speculative purposes.

Thus, the context of any experience, its entourage of "others," while in one way competing with it for attention, in another way adds to its meaning. There is such a thing as a distracting and ruinous rivalry among objects of possible attention: there is also a kind of otherness which, affording relief and distance, re-enters into and enhances the meaning of the object. As in Mr. Gilbert Chesterton's experience, one must leave Battersea in order to perceive Battersea. In Battersea, among his trunks, he declares, "I am going to Battersea—by way of Rome, Vienna, Saint Petersburg." After dead mechanism, the chief enemy of meaning is repetition, routine, mere quantitative prolongation. Intelligent living on a limited subject matter tends to kill its own savor; for its business is to "know its business," that is, to produce a set of classifications which provide for everything; but once these classifications have been successfully set up, the price of success being the destruction of novelty, the processes of living are reduced to tedium.

Now this possibility of seeing the particular as it is, is also the possibility of conceiving it improved or varied. The mental excursion which through contrast illuminates the essence of the thing brings also the critical imagination, wherein lie the seeds of fertility. For the fulcrum of fertility is that vision of the particular in which all that is accidental about it becomes salient: to see it as a factual specimen which might well be otherwise is the first step in actually devising a deviation, a novelty in the world.

Experience of an "other" is one of the conditions of invention, of still further otherness.

Hence we observe that the great ages of invention have often been ages of physical or mental exploration. The noblest products of human thought, civilizations, tend to throw over their members the spell of totality, and, therefore, of necessity: their peculiarities are not felt as peculiar, but under the hypnosis of invariable recurrence, they assume the air of axiomatic and universal validity. To escape from such a fixation, whether by travel or by trade or even by invasion, is like all liberations profoundly disturbing; but a due succession of such shocks of otherness is a favoring condition for the vitality of any culture, and, one suspects, a necessity. May something similar be true of our mental preoccupation with the more general traits of this one world, with its peculiarities of space, mass, energy, organization?

I believe we have no choice but to generalize our principle. Fertility in novelty is required if any continued experience is to retain such meaning as it has; still more so if it is to achieve such meaning as it is capable of. If this is true, then to every particular there should be an equally actual other. An empty imagination will not do, nor the mere logical category of otherness: the logical principle that to every particular "this" there is a conceivable "other" is only a blank permission to conceive such an other if one can. An actual and concrete "other world" would be the best condition for lively fertility of mind in regard to this one, if it were free from invidious rivalry.

Now imagination is always busy, making use of this logical permission, and presenting to us sketches, not alone of other languages, other lands, other geometries and algebras, but also of other selves, other lives, other worlds. It fills these logical schemes with imagery whose accidental character it recognizes—making them myths and symbols of what it regards real. It insists on only one literal ingredient of these fancies, namely, that its other world shall be genuinely other (transcendent) to whatever particular we can describe as "this"—the alternative being an eventual failure of fertility, and a value-law of entropy, threatening whatever values we now enjoy with a gradual trend to insalience, that is to say, to nothingness.

e) *Temporal otherness, or beyondness*

What we are tracing is the law that the context of an experience of value may be, and normally is, a contributing factor to its worth and not a competing or disparaging factor.

This remains true when the supposed context is an "other," in the sense of a succeeding segment of time, a "future life."

It is commonly said that duration has nothing to do with the value of an experience: it is not temporal prolongation but quality that counts. On this ground it is the aim of life to win some apprehension of the "eternal values," and with that attainment to be satisfied. Continuing to live adds nothing to the value of one's best moments; and to go on after those best moments into poorer ones is merely to degrade the total character of one's life. A longing for undying continuation is thus a sign of a certain lack of inner dignity, and indeed of unworthiness to continue, and the only way to be fit for immortality would be not to desire it.

If this were true, life ought to take the form of progress toward some climax of appreciation, followed at once by extinction. For to look back, even for a moment, at one's height, is to confess one's present decline. And there is indeed an aesthetic satisfaction in ending on one's best note, and a certain justice in the feeling that to a truly great experience there can be no sequel that is not a loss.

But why do we dread the sequel? Not because it is what it is—we know nothing about that—but because it is a something which intrudes upon the retrospect which belongs to a moment of elevation.

It is not the extinction of consciousness that the great experience demands, but a lengthy, unoccupied time in which to realize what has occurred. The notion that time has nothing to do with value is thus exactly contrary to the psychological law of meaning! The intense experiences may be brief, but they are long looked forward to and long remembered. Like a noble building, they demand an adequate vista; and consciousness labors to provide it by amplifying the time of its undisturbed contemplation.

It may be doubted whether there is not some contradiction in speaking of a great experience "at a moment." For to be assaulted by the presence of greatness is not to take it in; a mountain makes no immediate impression of vastness—it conspires with the illusions of distance to conceal its proportions, and we only know them through the journey and the climb. The law of value experience is similar; for our finite minds, if that which is noble is to be known, its apprehension must be built through a history of lesser things, and must be remembered and related to them all.

To cease, then, at the point of any attainment is to lose the full meaning of that attainment. From the mere logic of meaning, then, there is no moment at which conscious existence could appropriately cease. And if there were such a thing as an "eternal value" accessible to us mortals, it would rightly call for unlimited time for its realizing.

f) *Continuity of historic reference*

Closely connected with this matter of duration is that of the historic continuity of the inquiring self. Meaning accumulates, much as a question persisted in through time accumulates its answer. Some questions are inseparable from individual existence, such as the questions "What am I?," "What is the world?," "What is the good?" Personal identity is made by the identity (not the similarity) of these questions over gaps of consciousness.

The continuity of memory does not itself constitute the identity of selfhood, but the pertinence of the contents of memory to its continued questions. The nature of selfhood shows itself in the nature of memory; for the self makes it own memory by its instinctive selection of what it deems significant, as data for its ultimate answers.

We were saying that among these remembered events are the notable joys and elevations of experience. This is half the story. We remember also the notable depressions and evils. It is not that we consciously choose to remember them; we may prefer to cover them with a veil, but they remain as unwelcome guests. The psychoanalyst speaks, at times, as though they maintained themselves against our will; but no event has any power to continue its own being. As an event it is gone and only the mind can retain it, but it may be retained by the spontaneous loyalty of the reflective self to its own problem. The pains, sorrows and shames of life—what we summarily call its "evils"— are precisely those aspects of experience which are not understood—not yet understood. The pleasures and insights offer clues to the meaning of life; as momentary they do not constitute that meaning, but they intimate what it is like. Hence in memory suffering and evil are juxtaposed with them as the burden which they eventually have to lift, not exclude. Together they constitute the question which life—not so much contains—as is! How do these evils and these goods belong together?

Now it is a truism that this answer cannot come to another questioner. In many points posterity will know what to us is unknown, and we are willing that our successors shall have that knowledge which is the tool for their own day's work. But my question—unless it is answered to me who ask it—is not answered at all. Someone else may and will carry on the general problem involved, and may get the general answer involved in my problem. But these questions of meaning and truth are not generalities merely; they are issues arising out of particular experience, and, divorced from that experience, that memory, that hardship, that injustice, they are empty.

Meaning grows through time, and it cannot grow great, or grow at all, by lopping off the first containers as if they could be decanted into another series. The early history of a question is part of the question, and the loss of the beginnings of the questions put to the world would be an irreparable loss of meaning. Continuance of personal questions is thus demanded for meaning, not merely because the questioner wants the future but because the future wants the questioner; it will always need its own past in order to be itself, just as the number series would be falsified as a counting system if the first n numbers were lopped off.

From these principles it is evident that the prevalent

notion that interest in another world is intrinsically a subtraction from interest in this world is the precise reverse of the normal situation. It is true that men have often made a disease of other-worldliness, mooning and imagining and stealing their affections away, and deferring effort for justice, and abandoning this world as a rotting hulk. These, the fallacies of pure detachment, we have seen enough of.

We remark only that they cannot be cured by an effort to abolish the context of "this" world, in the supposition that the effort for human justice would then be intensified. This is the fallacy of all humanism and of all the current Marxist hostility to an other-worldly religion. The effort for justice remains in full vigor only when men are supposed ends-in-themselves, endowed with the dignity of right, free and of limitless possibility. Draw your line around the man at his death, cut across all the lines of his aspiration, snuff out all his major questions, quash all his claims, declare all his unfinishedness a zero to the cosmos, and the nerve of all this concern for justice is also cut. Humanism tries to borrow for its humanitarian zeals an inherent worth in the individual human being which its premises forbid him to have. Without his continuance, his present cannot hold its own meaning and worth.

VI

THE MAKING OF A SELF

THERE is an aspect of Plato's meditations which appears instructive to me at this point. For the most part Plato inadvertently confirms the general impression that a vivid interest in immortality tends to the disparagement of the present existence. To him, this would be no sign of error; for in his views, this mode of life ought to be disparaged, just in so far as it is actually imperfect. He reflects the views of the Orphics and Pythagoreans according to which the soul, imprisoned in this body, would be more itself without the intrusions of sense and the contaminations of desire. Plato's proofs of immortality have received severe handling from subsequent philosophy, beginning with Aristotle, whose convincing picture of the organic union of soul and body made it clear that the unitary and simple entity which Plato proved invulnerable could not be a concrete surviving person. But before Aristotle, Plato himself argued against Plato. For if the union of the soul with the body is, as he claims, a misfortune and a fall, there is no sufficient reason for birth, and still less reason, once the soul by death has escaped from the toils of the body, for resuming empirical existence. Human existence, however, is clearly not a meaningless affair for Plato. We can only conclude, then, that there is an unfinished element in his reasoning.

It is here that the myths of Plato are superior to his arguments, and represent more fully the real Plato. His convictions are there; his arguments are afterthoughts. Let us then condense, with large editorial liberties, the purport of pertinent Platonic myth on this point.

The soul after death spends an ample time in the underworld, passing through various adventures and tests. The time comes when it must return to earth. It must choose a new lot among a number which are spread out before it. It chooses on the basis of those preferences which have been bred in it by its former life or lives, and especially as impressed by their disadvantages. It chooses something different! Then, passing through the plain of forgetfulness, it is shot forth to a new birth in the type of career of its own choosing.

The presumption of the picture is that this new lot in turn fails to bring the satisfaction which the soul had promised itself. Hence a new stage of value judgment, a new death, a new choice, another experiment in living.

In this process, with its touch of irony, we see at once that empirical living has acquired a positive meaning for Plato. Life is to be regarded as *a stage of self-education in the soul's grasp of the meaning of the good.* It is an experimental inquiry. Its method is dialectical, as befits the education of a free agent. It is granted in each life what it thinks it wants, and so is led to a perception of what it more truly wants, by successively rectifying its imperfect hypotheses. This process may require for an average soul some ten thousand years; but the philosopher who makes a business of it—Plato playfully suggests—

may work it through in three thousand! In any case, it is only through the assumption that the process is to be completed that the segment, this life, acquires its meaning. Without the whole, the part remains meaningless.

In this respect the Platonic myth exemplifies the principle of meaning which I here present: immortality normally an addition to the significance of present living, not a subtraction from it. With the aid of Aristotle and subsequent thinkers we can give a greater concreteness to this meaning of the empirical element in thought. We see that Plato was wrong in supposing that there could be any soul without body or any perfection of idea without a temporal exemplification. We see that existence is itself an element of perfection, and that the Idea at work in the facts is more ideal than the Idea apart from the facts. And by dint of this we may venture another version of that total meaning of the time process which lends itself to the parts.

One is learning what it is to be a self, not merely by trying various careers and gaining wisdom through failure, but by building a self, a process which is an effort toward embodying reality.

It will be agreed by all varieties of thought that, in some sense, we are, in what we call "experience," actively dealing with reality. The meaning of this term "reality" is elusive, and many prefer to drop it. But no one proposes a substitute, and for our present purpose we require no more recondite significance than the difference we all recognize between dealing with shams which collapse on testing, and dealing with veritable beings which survive all tests; or between false notions which we try to shed and true notions which we try to acquire; or between partial insight with which we may be culpably content, and a judgment stable and complete, which may require relentless effort. If reality is that factor in experience which persistently corrects false or partial views, we are, in a sense which we all understand, dealing with reality. Now in this process we are becoming real ourselves. This, I think, is the point of the matter.

No doubt a certain reality may be attributable to consciousness, by the mere fact that it exists. Descartes is quite right in pointing out that the thinking self cannot repudiate its own part in existence. But in my view, the reality which the self has at any time is a tentative basis upon which to acquire or achieve reality at another level.

What, then, is meant by the achieving of reality? We become real in proportion as we know truth and get rid of illusions. Yes; but when do we know truth? We are never sure of it until we can make it. The principle of our knowledge is the same as that of God's knowledge as Lactantius describes it: *solus potest scire qui fecit*. And if we look at the process of living with this idea in mind, we can see that we are, in fact, perpetually remaking the world, and in so doing coming to understand it, and, through understanding, becoming more completely real.

Our first remaking is in memory. Our world is given to us, let us say, in sense perception and in impressions of connection or structure among these points; there is nothing we thus perceive which we cannot in principle recall. But how much of what we perceive do we actually recall? A few traits which strike us as essential and important. How good is this selective judgment? Try to draw the face of your best-known friend in his absence, and you are forcibly reminded that your memory has done far less than a perfect work—you are by so much below "reality" in your grasp. In some such way as this my activity, because it must be concrete, is the continuous test of my conceptions. In so far as this process is successful, my conceptions become real in the sense of being adequate to reality; and the proof of it is that I can reproduce what I have first of all merely observed and accepted.

Now I cannot create an object without at the same time creating the type of domain or world room in which it exists, and which enters into its existence. My creation thus takes the typical form of the work of art, in which I do bring forth out of my mental resources another space and time, another collocation of events and persons, structural lines and processional fragments out of another world; my work of "fiction" is my essay in reality, and my product passes judgment on myself. So far as I am, in my consciousness, fantastic, sentimental, brutal, shallow, thrill-greedy, romantic, morbid or otherwise unreal, my novel or my play, my picture or my song, will betray and advertise these characters: and with enough docility, I may have the fortune to see them myself, and move beyond them. So far as I have grasped the nature of things, I will have given it back in a new version, but with an addition—the improvement which is "my idea" and which has never been thought before.

Among such creations there is one which is every man's product, and in a peculiar sense each one's own deed, namely, this empirical self. Every decision helps to make it; for every act has as its object (a) a change in the external world and (b) a conception of one's self as author of that change. However much the self begins its career as a product of previous lives and of society, the excursive self which I send out into the world of events begins in time to bear the character of my handiwork. There is a large amount of failure in it and evasion of the hard work of becoming what I conceive a man to be; but, for better or worse, it is my product, and in making it I have become clearer in my notions of what reality in human nature is. I am prepared to make a better specimen!

If one were to conceive this life, then, as a sort of *apprenticeship in the capacity to create*, in which one's advancement measures one's degree of attained reality, one would be closely interpreting the empirical facts in the light of an incessant striving, which may be largely subconscious. And, in particular, I am learning how to create a self.

We are inclined, in retrospect, to judge the meaning of a life, our own or others, somewhat in terms of achievement. We recount what a man has done. We praise it, in so far as some ideal has been worked into the fabric of human history. We conceive life as engaged, in so far as it is well bent, in the wholehearted service of ideal aims, some of which, in the providence of nature and society, get embodied in human work. But there are accidents in achievement and injustices in this retrospect. Is the accomplished deed, after all, the measure of the man, set as it is in a perishable and fickle stream of human eventuality? There are few eulogies which are satisfied with their catalogues of accomplishment, they seem uneasily aware that this is not the main thing. The count of what and how much seems an external attachment, only partly attributable to the man. Are there not some who in such terms achieve nothing? And are they therefore worthless? And must a man think of himself in these terms? What is more melancholy than to feel bound to take the public view of one's self? Do we exist in order to act? Or do we act in order to exist? Our deepest instinct would suggest that what a man has not yet attained may be vastly more important than what he has performed; and that what he is, is more important than either. His true achievement is the degree of reality embodied in his character.

In point of fact, is there anything which more positively acts than what a man is? The reflexive self makes felt its continuous, inevitable, unuttered comment on the insufficiencies of the self of achievement, and whoever witnesses the deed, sees also the sign of that dissatisfaction, which continues to aim beyond it. The true meaning of a deed is what it means to the self which performs it; without this self the deed has no meaning at all; it is the "being" which attends and sustains all "doing" that assigns to it whatever depth of meaning it may have. In this sense there is no meaning at all except in the being of the self.

And if this self vanishes, and all like it, meaning vanishes out of the world. No achievement can keep the person alive, but the continuance of the person is a guaranty that such values as that shall not reduce to nothing. It is the person who perpetuates the achievement, not the achievement the person.

This estimate of meaning has fallen into disrepute with the spread of the pragmatic philosophy, which has no ultimate estimate of being except in terms of doing. In the proposal we here make we have assigned a place to pragmatism, since active attachment is necessary to a sound detachment, and one must work in order to be real. But we make being primary.

At the center of the healthy spirit there is a preference, hard to explain on any philosophy of deed-adjustment—

a preference for the tough passages of experience when, through them, one sees the starker truth and rouses himself to meet it. This is the spirit of the old Stoic invitation to pain, "Strike, sacred Reality!" It is also the spirit of the poet Rilke when he said, "I am often surprised to see how ready I am to give up everything hoped for, for the Real, even when it is grievous." [1] Not surely for love of the grievous, but for that greater sense of *being* which can absorb the grievous.

Now the embarrassment of considering being as the substance of meaning is that it is just this which death appears to annihilate. One's deeds live after him; what one is, or was, remains only as a flavor or aroma which passes with the personal impression. There are, to be sure, habit-ridden scholars who continue to amass knowledge to the day of their death, as if forgetting that it, of all things, must perish with the brain. There are devotees like the dying Proust who continue to discipline their souls to the very end. Bosanquet conceived the soul as the finest product and soul-building the major occupation of the universe; and yet just this soul he thought the vulnerable and perishable thing. Is there not in this blind cultivation of the self a certain fanaticism, a subjective momentum, a desperate drawing of water from failing wells —or perhaps a certain quixotic disdain of sense in the arbitrary interest of holding one's plume intact? Why should one who can no longer *do* insist on *being?*

It may be blindness, or the high gesture of the sporting spirit, still conscious in anticipation of the imagined admiring glances of surviving men; or if going out alone— as the last man might—preferring to leave on the night

[1] *"Es wundert mich manchmal, wie bereit ich alles Erwartete aufgebe für das Wirkliche, selbst wenn es arg ist."*

the echoes of a defiant lover of Stoic virtue, as if, parodoxically, the unconscious world would have to remember! A futile subjective conceit, or a dogma of aesthetic preference! But also, it may be wisdom and a deeper sense for the realities of the world. In my view it is this deeper thing. We care for being more than for achievement, because being, in this sense, is an enduring potentiality; and this can only signify potentiality for further life. The self that is produced, one's dated creation, this self vanishes; the reflective self, having attained a measure of reality in that creative deed, is ready for another stage, not excluding the first, in knowing and embodying the depth of being.

VII

CONCLUSION: MYSTIC AND REALIST

OUR conclusion is not a metaphysical doctrine. It is a proposal about certain conditions which are necessary if human life is to have an adequate meaning, whether for the modern man or for any other man.

One such condition is that human life must have a supplement, a perspective of perpetuity. Another, that this present existence may be considered as an invitation to take on reality, understanding by this term not the phenomenal and passing reality which we have in hand but a complete and radical reality, an equivalence to whatever powers there are in the world which environs us.

To become real in any such sense would be an endless task, requiring endless time; yet it is a direction which we instinctively take and in the course of the human span achieve something of. Without any prior weighing of better or worse, we drive as we can toward "objectivity" of mind and judgment. We fear illusion as the primordial plague, and piece by piece get rid of our private stock of vanities, fancies, superstitions about ourselves and the world. Punished as these follies are by failure and chagrin, we are compelled as well as drawn toward a deeper genuineness in observing, laboring, imagining, planning. The "real" in the world outside us patiently corrects our subjectivities and errors: and by dint of this, the pain and labor of "experience," we arrive at an entertainment of relative truth; we become relatively "real."

Could we fully attain reality, the survival of death would necessarily follow; for it belongs to the real that it *lasts*. But since what we can attain is only a degree and kind of realness, there is only a possibility that this degree and kind may carry through the crises of death. We here assert no more than this possibility.

It may well be that the survival of death is not a foregone conclusion, as if each person with or against his will were doomed to everlastingness. The soul is certainly not endowed, as Plato thought, with the fixed, substantial degreeless reality of the atom. It possesses, we think, not immortality but immortability. It depends upon itself what degree of realness it comes to possess. Immortality may be "put on"; one may also put on mortality. The soul may resolve to take the present, partial scene of things as final, and may by determined action upon that hypothesis make it true for its own experience. It is the nemesis of an imperfect realism that its illusions become its effective reals.

The primary evidence for this view of things lies in experience, an aspect of experience which the modern man shares with the primitive, an intuition which it may be difficult for him to single out, but which he need not have lost nor in the fullest light of science forgo. I refer to that deep-lying innocence of the mind (its "negative wholeness") whereby it carries on its living *as though there were to be no temporal end* of its being.

It is this innocence, challenged by the factual limits of life, which brought forward the first crude doctrines of the survival of death, and lent to the hard existence of aboriginal folk a glimmer of significance. Without this same perception our own lives, far richer in spotwise satisfactions, are poorer than theirs and drift toward a zero of meaning.

So far as we can recover this our own underlying sense of unlimited ongoing, we can recognize at once how far from truth is the fear that the fringe of otherness which supplements this life—the "other world"—is hostile to full-minded attention to this present business. The measure of possible detachment from this occupation is at the same time the measure of possible attachment to it. It is *by way of* that whole-vista that I am able to value this part. The simplicity of the child allows it wholehearted-ness in every moment: the mature man cannot retain that childish simplicity, but he may retain its rational equivalent. Note carefully that the child is *not* treating his present moment "as if it were all"; for anyone who regards the present moment as all, as if he were saying of it, "This which I now have is the end: let me make the most of it," is incapable of wholehearted absorption in that moment: his mind is obsessed by the fact of limit or boundary, and what might be beyond it. To be able to give oneself whole-heartedly to the present one must be persistently aware that it is *not all*. One must rather be able to treat the present moment as if it were engaged in the business al-lotted to it by that total life which stretches indefinitely beyond.

For most purposes of experience, it is better to leave this supplement of life in the simple and pseudo-negative form of "no cessation, no absolute finitude," rather than attempt to grasp the total purport of existence in any phrase such as "knowing things as they are" or "attaining reality." For as we consciously define our ultimate end, we burden all action with a double purpose: each act has its own immediate aim, but then it also contributes (or should contribute) to that ultimate end. Indeed I ought to consider my act primarily in that latter light, and so, after all, my wider aim threatens to detract from my present aim. This has been the bane of all pietisms, that every act had not only its own burden, but also the burden of God's glory, or some other aspect of the cosmic process. Life was dignified by the nobility of its horizon, but also solemnized, and its spontaneity impaired.

Thus the philosopher, like the theologian, seems doomed to intrude upon the normal simplicities of human behavior an extraneous consciously ideal aim. He is bound to do this: he can only meet the problem of meaning which life sets in terms of conceptions, even while acknowledging the flimsiness of the intellectual cages in which he endeavors to imprison what always escapes formulation. But he is equally bound to indicate the position of the *mystic*, who escapes this difficulty.

It is the special function of the mystic to remind us of the risks of all definition, while adhering to an equally vigorous insistence that there is something there which we must forever try to define. Maintaining a rigidly skeptical aloofness toward all "conceptions" (except one or two!), he is all the more emphatic about those meager assertions in which he feels himself impregnable. Such as these: that *there is a meaning* in the whole of things; that we are always dimly aware of it; and that it is possible to raise the dim awareness to a firm immediate conviction.

This first assertion, that there is meaning, is a thin assertion—a mere "that" without a "what"—such as mystics delight in to the provocation of all who desire concreteness. Yet its very thinness insures that it will never get into the way of present action. And it may well be the most important assertion to set into our foundations. For if it is certain that there is a meaning, it becomes reasonable to spend a lifetime or more in the search for it, and to reject those negations repeatedly put forward by the confusion of philosophic voices or by the perplexities of one's own experience. If it is *not* certain that there is a meaning, the zeal for finding it might reasonably at some time give out. We are naturally disposed to give life the benefit of the doubt and to take the pragmatic attitude, "Act *as if* life were worth living"—as good a risk as any to push out on: we can adhere to this in all good faith as long as courage holds out; but if indeed we are acting purely on a working-hypothesis, sustained by ourselves, we must be prepared to meet facts which will require a negative verdict. The mystic rejects all such pragmatism; he has his certainty: and because of it, he is forever debarred, and would debar others, from indulging in the luxury of despair.

If we ask him how he can be certain, the mystic refers us to that which is always better than proof, immediate experience. It is that same thread of experience that we have been following, the primitive innocence which asserts "No end," the simplicity of the child's absorption, but with this additional and positive character, an indefinable awareness of ultimate worth in what he now does. He declares (with full awareness of the paradox) that this distant and elusive meaning is always dimly felt as an inseparable quality of ongoing experience, too close to us to be clearly discerned but also too close to be doubted.

If we disavow any such experience on our own part, he displays the same invincible and preposterous assurance about our experience and the experience of others as he has about his own, as if he had access to the unities which run through and beneath the separate pools of selfhood. He appeals if necessary from our ordinary consciousness to subconsciousness; he asks us to witness that in our very elemental hold on biological existence a vein of enjoyment and a vein of suffering lie close together, each binding us to life more strongly because of the presence of the other. He hints that there are arts of attention which, fanning this central value sense into a strong illumination, may reveal for an instant the ties which connect the present self with the uncharted field of universal meaning, and leave this vision as a permanent conviction of the conscious self. He points out that there are moments in which this awareness comes to the fore, and certifies not alone the passing event but all others. There are occasions for every man in which the usual sense of being a very minor factor in events disappears into a new sense of validity and freedom: "I can take care of *this* event; what is before me to do, I *can* do, and to that extent budge all the facts of the universe from within this small focus of action." At this moment one ceases to weigh the various alternative means to his end; he ceases to doubt the validity of his ends. "Only one thing is worth doing, that is supremely worth doing, and it has ceased to be hard to do, you cannot say why." [1] The self has projected its concern quite beyond the rim of its private

[1] *C. E. Montague: A Memoir,* p. 299. See also his short story "Action" for an illustration of this experience.

enclosure, and leaning hard against the outer resistance, like Samson against the pillars, feels it *give*! This is freedom in the concrete, the genuine, and full-fledged freedom: in that experience one knows himself to be as real as the outside world. One knows, too, that the meaning of things is presently felt by him, as running through that act of his.

Taken by himself, the mystic is likely to be an encouraging person, but also a tantalizing person, running a risk at least as grave as that of the philosophical definer, that of mistaking subjective confidence for objective truth. Yet he is no mere mythologist; he is one who sees and calls on others to see. In my judgment he is right in his primary assertions, that there is a total meaning in things, and that we are all dimly aware of it, and may thus be certain that it exists. Unless there is an immediately felt meaning there is no meaning at all: no future meaning could compensate for a complete absence of meaning in the present moment; and whatever meaning life may come to possess hereafter must be simply the ampler interpretation of the meaning which it now has. I could not seek it, had I no present clue to that which I am seeking. I could not yearn for what is not here, unless yearning could contemplate that which is missing, and in contemplating enjoy its image.

At the same time, this immediate certainty is not enough. If living were so much its own always available and sufficient apology there would be no reason for a program of action and change. Taking him strictly at his word, the mystic, like the Stoic, would have to refer the whole business of daily life to some inferior mechanism, such as the conventional round of duties. In point of biographical fact, he is not usually thus consistent. He commonly finds himself, in practical affairs, a strenuously effective individual, like some Savonarola or Eckhart or Loyola. Sometimes he condescends to this "realism" with an uneasy sense of duplicity, as if he ought to be an alien in this world of fact. More often he perceives that the art of life must unite, in some fashion, its realistic with its mystical phases, and seeks some further understanding of this union. As a matter of practical program, we all tend to alternate between the two.

We must be realists in action, definite, analytical, responsible, critical, separating good and evil, refusing to palliate or be reconciled to the violence, cruelty, and callousness of the world, concentrated on the task on hand and its object as if they were all-important, as if experience were to have just such value as by these efforts we can extract from it and no more.

And then, when through the very vehemence of our concentration the value and sense of what we are doing leak away from it, as tends to happen at the end of every day's work, we must become mystics in order to renew that sense of the whole which can shed its value down again on the parts. We have to recover, by some art or other, what Mencius called our "child's heart" and what Lao Tze called *Tao*, the nameless simplicity of being and outlook which confers proportion, unity and wholeness upon the distraught fragments of endeavor. These are but other names for that aboriginal hold on ultimate reality which, the mystic rightly says, is inalienable from human selfhood.

All normal living finds its sanity through some version of this alternation or rhythm. But alternation, a practical solution, is not an understanding. Can the realist include this mystic in his view, or can the mystic absorb the realist, or can some third view include both?

In the end, the mystic finds the reason for his realistic phase, though to explain it he resorts once more to myth. He feigns that since his action in time affects the fortunes of others beside himself, he has some particular thing to do *for them* (and not alone for his own development as a real) though he knows not what it is. In this sense his active life is an infinite network of crossings of paths, in each of which crossings or encounters with others he transmits to them such reality as he has, until then, attained. Life thus contains a series of *rendezvous* with Destiny; and all living, full of potential adventure, has the significance of preparation for such encounters. The peril of living is that one may miss the meeting with Destiny, or fail through unfitness to do that which was then and there to be done.

Confucius, who like many men of great reticence on metaphysical questions has been reputed an agnostic, was in this sense a mystic. When his life had been endangered by an attack at K'uang he said in effect "Heaven (Tien) has appointed me to teach this doctrine; until I have done so, what can the people of K'uang do to me?" Many a mystic (and many a soul not so designated) has retained this sense that his life, with its many pseudo-accidental entanglements, is woven into some total purpose, his *agendum* par excellence. In Hutchinson's story, *If Winter Comes*, there are the two inveterate chess players, Fergus and Saber. Fergus is one who insists (like a proper mystic) that his life has a particular purpose, though he does not know what it is. Saber confronts him with realistic skepticism, and the dialogue runs on somewhat as follows:

Saber: "How can you pursue a purpose if you don't know what it is?"

Fergus: "How can you try for a solution of a chess problem if you don't know what it is?"

Saber: "But you know that there *is* a solution."

Fergus: "That's it; and you know that there *is* a purpose!"

Whatever may be the play of poetry within this myth of the *agendum*, there is a basis of literal truth which the philosopher will sometime extract and confirm. It contains at least this: That, just as a work of art—if it is a good work—means the universe, while in turn, the universe means *it*, exists for such as it, so life, always tending toward futurity without end, means that ultimate goal, but in turn the ultimate goal means *it*. If there is no total meaning, none of the daily details can conserve importance. *If there is an eternal meaning*, there is nothing better in all futurity than some of the things which human life, here in the middle of time, may contain. If there is an absolute sense of existence, life has nothing better to do, at any time, than to move toward the human encounter in which real may speak to real, and in so doing give alms to the Absolute. And while the "attainment of reality" is a general aim, identical for everybody and hence giving no special reason for my existence or yours, this conception of the personal *agendum*, as containing what the universe means, lends to each self and to each deed the weight of the world's expectancy and need, which I alone, in this pass, can meet.

Thus the mystic view absorbs the realist view: the true mystic has to be, and can be, a realist, as the realist cannot be a mystic without cracking his realistic frame of being. The mystic performs the miracle which the realist requires but cannot perform for himself—he renews the ever-ebbing values of the daily task by restoring amplitude-of-horizon to the detail of living.

I say the mystic within us performs this recurrent miracle, but only through what he sees; he relies throughout on corroboration from the nature of things as they are. He is invoking at every point, perhaps through symbol and myth, the greater miracle, far beyond his solitary power—that of bringing dawn back into the sunset, the endless otherness of life into the crux of death.

In so doing, he holds himself responsible to whatever new light the persistent and legitimate realism of mankind, through science, logic, and cosmology, brings to the wider frame of existence. This cold light may banish his vision; it may give that vision its needed literality of support. In either case, the true mystic will never evade the task, now before us, which imperils all his hope; for unless he has truth, he has nothing.

PART IV

INTERLUDE:
NEWER PERSPECTIVES
OF COSMOS
AND DESTINY

AGE OF ANALYSIS

THROUGH what has gone before, there may, I trust, have emerged a sense that the question of personal survival of death—surely the most postponable of human questions, endlessly deferred in the inescapable thicket of "the day's business"—is itself an inescapable part of "the day's business."

For no thinking creature can live without some image of the Whole in which its activity is engaged: even a cat, before settling down to a meal, makes sure of its exits. Our human Whole-idea, noninsistent because omnipresent, is incessantly at work. And within this outlook, what we consider the ultimate destiny of persons to be, ourselves and others—whether extinction or something else—plays a crucial and equally silent role.

Once we recognize the pervasiveness of the issue of survival, we become responsible to ourselves, if to no others, for examining its possibility, with whatever critical equipment we can command. The mystic, I have said, will be the last to shrink from the task; but only the realist can measure its full difficulty.

For such an examination, the present period—let us say the half-century now ending—is peculiarly propitious. It is so, just because the prevailing Winds of Doctrine are adverse. It is only the firmly skeptical temper that can meet the severe realism of the need for light on this issue.

In this period, there has been no lack of new and powerful thinking pertinent to the character of things-as-a-whole. Willy-nilly, while avoiding the name as the plague, this era has been "metaphysical"—i.e., bent on passing summary judgment on What Is. Whether through undercutting older foundations of physical science, or through ruthless depth-exploring of human psychology, or through philosophical analyses disposed to deal rudely with delusions—under which head current "idealisms" are by preference included—its theme has been *the cosmological frame of human life*; and under its scrutiny, this frame has altered its traditional contours before our eyes. These alterations have been such as to reduce the significance of the local and fleeting human episode implacably toward zero.

With the sciences, the spirit of literature and the arts remains in essential sympathy; its wings, too, beat against customary barriers and equally discount customary human prides and hopes. It calls for naturalness, if not naturalism, and therewith for a deep-drinking reappraisal of the raw and primitive, sometimes bordering on the pathological but essentially explorative and courageous. In its vigor, it strikes out many an inestimable flash of light.

Flashes, to be sure, are not enough. They are seldom sure of their own direction: coherence and welding force must be brought from outside, and at a certain ruthless distance from the tempers of revolt. With these conditions our "Age of Analysis" becomes a mine of opportunity. We here touch on three of its proposals notably adverse to the notion of survival.

I

A BROAD AGNOSTICISM

In all its thoughtful dealings with our human situation, the present century has been remarkable for the prominence of questions of logical analysis, of the theory and psychology of knowledge. How and what can we human beings know? What do the accidents of language, and those other accidents of subconscious impulse, do to form and malform our thinking? May not semantic criticism on one side and psychoanalysis on another relieve future mankind forever of the futilities of metaphysics? And since our problem of survival is definitely metaphysical, our present inquiry would be one of the first futilities to be eliminated.

It remains possible that the common man is still untouched by the suspicion that any semantic transformation of the to-him-empirical question of a future life could dispose of it as meaningless. One might, with perhaps some faint *méchanceté*, quote Bertrand Russell at this point, to the effect that philosophy is concerned "with the meaning of the world, not solely with the meaning of sentences." [1] And the meaning of the world to man cannot

[1] *The Hibbert Journal*, July, 1956, p. 320. His words are: "My fundamental aim has been to understand the world as well as may be. . . .

be wholly separable from the meaning of human life to the world.

But on serious thought regarding survival, the total impact of current analysis has been not to dismiss the question, but to replace an earlier confident affirmation, and equally confident denial, with the judgment on the part of both realist and mystic that "we really cannot know about it." This is true in quarters in which we have hitherto been able to expect decisive conclusions, con and pro—from naturalists and realists on one side, from the religious mind on the other.

So discerning a writer as the late W. P. Montague, disposed in some respects to a materialist groundwork in his philosophy, and inclining to relate mental phenomena to the puzzling physical concept of potential energy, has written that "the ancient questions are beyond the power of science to answer. If answered at all, they will be answered by mystic faith or by metaphysical speculation, not by anything that is proved or even implied by the ascertained facts of either psychology or physics." And as for metaphysical speculation itself, "philosophy cannot resolve the question that religion meets by faith." [2] So, generally, in the current literature of naturalism, instead of the former firm *a priori* denial of the possibility of survival, in which Professor Corliss Lamont now holds an outstandingly clear position, we find room for an acceptance of residual mystery in the structure of the universe calling for a final modesty of the mind, and an aversion to the universal negative.

But we are now told that it is not the world that we are to try to understand but only sentences." It is the later *Wittgenstein* that he has in mind, together with Neurath and Hempel "and Carnap at one time."

[2] *Columbia University Quarterly,* March, 1933.

On the other hand, the faith with which Montague thus credits religion is today strongly affected by the modern antipathy to other-worldliness. Without pressing the question whether there is or is not a Heaven in which the will of God is eternally done, the burden of the contemporary prayer of faith is that this will, at any rate, "be done on earth." And with this shift of emphasis, there has come a growing recognition that the natural will of man, quite apart from the generally abandoned threat of Hell, has capacities for self-criticism and self-discipline which render the "will of God" something far different from an alien and external Law. The natural ambition to do one's living well is as much a part of original human nature as is original sin. The issue between Confucius and Calvin— "man is by nature good," "man is by nature evil"—is commonly resolved today, whether by realist or by mystic, in the judgment that man is by nature both one and the other. Prone to follow his own immediate impulse, he can recognize that following as "sinful" when, and only when, *he himself* entertains the wider aim by which impulse is criticized.[3] If self-interest is natural, the persuasive goals offered to every growing individual by his social context, lifting his horizons far beyond the limits of self-only, are equally natural, just in so far as life-with-others is each man's own natural medium. The appeal to rightness of life as based on a divine command thus tends to identity with the appeal of an idealized human society; and this in turn with what one's own sense of values recognizes as intrinsically right.

[3] Dr. Lim Boom Keng, formerly president of the University of Amoy, settled the matter as follows: "Calvin is right; man is by nature evil, for children are naturally selfish. But Confucius and Mencius are also right; for as children grow up they have by nature the disposition to overcome their own selfishness."

And so far as this is true, the other world *loses its unique importance as source of moral law.* There is a this-worldly Beyond, which provides the needed scope. There are indeed few human beings untouched by a present and lively interest—rational or irrational—in doing something "for posterity," regardless of whether their own death will wholly veil from their ken the fortunes of posterity. The simple fact is that man has always lived for ends transcending his own life span, just so long as he retains respect for that human beyond. As Whitehead reminds us, "Certainly Regulus did not return to Carthage, with the certainty of torture and death, cherishing any mystic notions of another life—either a Christian Heaven or a Buddhist Nirvana. He was a practical man, and his ideal aim was the Roman Republic flourishing in this world. This aim transcended his individual personality. . . ." [4] In principle, this is not an exceptional state of mind: it may be considered a human development of the vertebrate disposition to sacrifice for offspring. Who would forgo the enjoyment of human affection, of caring and helping in present fact, and in imagination through an indefinite future, solely because one's self is to end in death?

And apart from this human Beyond, when we speak of "intrinsic values"—say of beauty or truth, abstract or embodied—they are none the less eternal because we who momentarily breathe their air shall later cease to breathe. While we live their joy endures as part of our own dimension; and the fact that they are capable of everlastingness makes us participants, during our brief span, in their freedom from limit. With this recognition, realist and mystic tend to converge in accepting the visible terminus.

For in its clearest-cut naturalism the modern temper

[4] *Adventures of Ideas*, p. 373.

is not without its capacity for "a free man's worship" of whatever it can glimpse of perfection. The dignity of such worship may be the greater for its deliberate acceptance of finitude, seizing eternity as it were in passing, even in passing *out*. And for its part, the religious mind does on the whole today acknowledge this natural human capacity for self-transcendence [5] as its own kin. Without dismissing the idea of immortality, it is less disposed to dwell on that idea as a necessary postulate of the moral life. Men can live for the enduring good without demanding their own endurance.

*   *   *

And so far as survival, and the future destiny of the soul in Judgment, cease to be the major fulcrums of religious appeal, there spreads an attitude, not of negation, but let me say of half-belief, a *conventional affirmation* which is a half-skepticism, tending to pervade the entire fabric of religious observance.

This predicament, an uncomfortable twilight of faith, has its profound pathos, especially affecting the quality of services for the dead. This pathos derives from the twofold nature of the ceremonial attention which human societies from early times have given to the event of disposing of the dead. Each such ceremonial is first of all an expression of feeling, and as such a moral need. At the same time, the expression is shaped by some current myth with theoretical content. The myth is itself a social institution, not put forward as a thesis requiring or even admitting rational defense: it is a carrier of the essential emotions of grief, gratitude, honor, and hope, and as such it expects the general assent of conformity.

[5] Cf. Robert Ulich's powerful survey, *The Human Career*, 1955.

And though the civilized world has gone far toward distinguishing between literality and symbol, something of the ancient predicament remains: while the total sense of the rite submerges its theoretical implications, yet the question of truth, now with sharper insistence, holds its subconscious requirement. And unless the implied assertions carry consent, *the emotion itself remains divided*, lacks clear integrity. This inner struggle constitutes a unique form of mental-moral suffering.

*   *   *

But take careful note of this suffering; for it contains a clear indication that agnosticism in regard to survival is not the last word. The fact that there is here an indelible question of inner veracity *precisely refutes* the suggestion of semantic analysis that there is *no truth to be had*. It is only because we know that there is a truth in the case that the faintest suspicion of a comforting self-deception can becloud the clarity of an intense emotion!

In this light, the *obstacle becomes an aid* to our work of thought. We recover our conviction that the metaphysical issue has its empirical significance and basis.

II

THE OBSTACLE
FROM ANTHROPOLOGY

AN AGE steeped like our own in the output of two centuries of eager anthropology cannot but find itself embarrassed with its riches in the folklore of the Beyond. The very profusion of the images proffered as metaphors of the substance of faith tends to discount the validity of any. For many a contemporary mind, The Golden Bough and its comrades and successors have sealed up all possible vistas of other-worldly conception. Our contemporary creeds, reticent as they have become, retain kinship with primitive and classical fancies, no part of whose imagery finds translation in sober judgment. At the same time, contemporary religion, mother of the principles of scientific method, has so far failed to bring forward a substitute: the poetry of the Apocalypse remains secure in our devotion to the magnificence of its symbolic vision. It is perhaps for philosophy to take upon itself the burden and the risk of bringing literality into the bewildering maze of speculation, while scientific anthropology contents itself with accumulating the phantasms of the race. As a science it passes no judgment on the validity of what it thus acquires.

Anthropology has, however, its responsibilities to sociology and psychology, as well as to the summary impression made by its treasury of fact, hardly to be dismissed as a magazine of human folly. The myths and observances have a function, else why their universality, their sacrificial persistence, their massive unanimity of aim?

I submit that we cannot dismiss as essentially meretricious this costly defiance of the finality of death, becoming at times so serious a subtraction from the material resources of living. Lippert, in his *Kulturgeschichte* finds an economic function for this drain: as an extension of *Lebensfürsorge* it requires, and engenders a habit of, excess production, and thus leads to a *capacity to save*—a reflection of possible interest in the history of capital! But the essential point is surely nearer the overt psychology of the participants: that man, even in his poverty, has been disposed to achieve a certain spot-wise munificence in order—with the aid of the ruling powers of the world— to preserve from pure perishing something of what he has seen as best. Death has occurred (or will occur): he does not contest the fact. But he *proposes to set up a permanence* in the midst of change, as at least a token of what deserves to endure, and is conceived as enduring.

It is to this deserving to endure, this "what ought to be," that our earlier discussions have drawn attention. Through all the anthropological assemblage of fantasy we discern an intelligible purpose, based on the unsupported assumption that there is some hidden bond between what ought to be and what is.

It is noteworthy, too, that in these his judgments of what deserves to last, man has been hindered by no palsy of relativity as between his own valuations and the divine valuations: in plain view of the broadest relativity in personal estimates of personal worth, man has assumed his capacity to achieve an absolute. (I note in passing that this assumption, which anthropology makes appear hazardous in the extreme, is inevitable in any religion holding that "God is good," implying that we know— beyond the danger of inversion—what "good" is. Especially in Christianity, the asserted kinship between God's nature as Father and our own can mean nothing else than that within our value judgments there is an element of universality. Our good cannot be God's evil, nor vice versa: otherwise, worship becomes a mockery. Then, what we most deeply cherish, he must cherish—such is the substance of that faith, and less explicitly, I presume, of all faith.)

It is undoubtedly true that man has passed too easily from what he conceives ought to be to what is. It remains possible that within this age-long and global manifesto of defiance there has spoken an intuition, needing and capable of rational defense. But it is here that the anthropological current in today's half-belief merges with a current deriving from the metaphysics of flux, namely, the conviction that in the world of actuality *nothing endures* —all things flow! A third and imperative obstacle to the thought of possible survival.

III

THE PHILOSOPHY
OF FLUX OR PROCESS

DURING the twenty years since our earlier discussion of the philosophy of flux in its bearing on human destiny (pp. 57f. above), the physical sciences, with philosophy in close partnership, have made advances toward answering the question, "What aspects of the material universe are in constant change, and what aspects have a certain durability?"

None of the thinkers whom we associate with the idea of change as primary metaphysical fact—Bergson, Alexander, Dewey, Whitehead—no one of them dispenses with every kind of stability. The logic of change forbids its establishment as rock-bottom basis of philosophy—is not the proposal self-contradictory? If change is king, there should be no rock-bottom. But further, change must be finite (for a first-rate example of the Meaningless, try to picture to yourself unlimited change) ; it has a finite rate, and a direction presumably formulable as a "law" of change. Perhaps the most revolutionary of the century's developments in physical theory is the simple equation putting an end to the conception of matter as changeless substance, whether as an association of eternal atoms or as "mass," $E = mc^2$. Yet that equation contains a "cosmic constant," and is wholly consistent with an ultimate "conservation" of some function of $m + E$. Our philosophers of flux, likewise, resort to certain permanences to conserve the durable meaning of their philosophies; yet those permanences are either themselves relative—passing equilibria among changes—or else conceptual rather than actual, as in Whitehead's order of "eternal entities." The actual remains a perpetual *becoming*, which is also, as with Locke, a "perpetual perishing."

And our concern with the destiny of persons is a concern with the actual—not disposed of by a discovered permanence whether of laws of change or of conceptual ideals. To allow that all the actual and concrete is perishable is a position strikingly in accord with current tempers. In our world-segment, at least, there is a marked appetite for passingness in the conditions of living. Witness the relatively rapid rate of demoding, the psychopathic demand for new models catered to by producers with appalling material waste, an apparent enjoyment of obsolescence with the excitement of readjustment and the forward look as the essence of life's interest. The speed of tiring, expressed, for example, in the intolerance toward repetition in music (Debussy and followers), imples a selective aversion toward durability, a penchant toward change for change's sake. A true philosophy must certainly have a place of honor for novelty; and if the present taste is valid, it must justify a swift and voluminous forgetfulness, as a necessary condition of the forward drive, impatient of the dragging encumbrance of past goods, impatient even of loyalty. The city that grows must be willing to tear down, and let the noble past, together with the dead past, bury its dead. It is thus fit-

ting to the time spirit that Descartes' two types of substance, thinking selves and extended plena, should be
abandoned; and that his (inconsistent) view that God
re-creates the world from instant to instant should survive—with the possible omission of the creating Deity—as
the incessant reception in new occasions of some part of
the impetus of perishing formations.

This technical and untechnical philosophy of flux,
though a genuine element in the *Zeitgeist*, is not itself a
passing phase: it is based on a valid illumination in which
all share. But what it here concerns us chiefly to note,
while accepting pervasive change, is *the use mankind
makes of the apparent permanences* of the world, in spite
of their illusory nature. The obelisk is indeed a pseudo-
permanence whose whole fabric is a truce in the decay of
form among countless changes held in fragile moving-
equilibrium. But the partial success of the intention of the
human spirit in using that delayed decay of form to
support an illusion of permanence—*that intention-and-
partial-success is not less part of the fact than the decay*.
Such revolt against total flux is at least part of the
meaning of "history"—I am inclined to say the essence
of it: it shows at least that mankind knows what it means
"to last." Where did it acquire that meaning? What experience gives us this idea?

This will to create the durable, returning again and
again to its pathetic and losing defiance of time-and-
change, is itself a durable expression of its own personal
identity, destined to establish its place in the changing
fabric of the event, through its care for other personal
identities like its own. Why should we, in our total picture of the world, give primacy to the always discoverable

processes of crumbling, the ant-hill-isms of analysis, when in man's intentions and work one near-permanence, failing, gives birth to others without end—as cities, always decaying, are always, as we were saying, torn down even in advance of decay, and *rebuilding*—in obedience to a resolute identity of purpose which persistently subdues process to itself?

This persistence of purpose is no doubt subjective: and as such is not enough of itself to refute the metaphysics of flux as a character of reality, *unless purpose itself is an ingredient of reality.* Man's universal, and universally futile, attempt to set up an Imperishable can be taken as empirical evidence that Flux is master, and purpose—at least human purpose—its plaything. If, as I am now doing, I take it as evidence to the exact contrary, it is with an unproved assumption that human purpose has an objective ally in the nature of things; and further that the *flux analysis is less than final on its own objective ground.* To this end, let me offer a few considerations.

What we can see at once is that change is known only with a simultaneous knowledge of nonchange *in the same context.* Time itself, involved in the concepts of change and change-rate, is a measurable amount only if its own lapse has an identifiable time point of beginning. For such identity, *memory* is indispensable: apart from memory, the past has no landmarks. With *recorded memory*, a purely human device (though using instruments which, turning time into contemporaneous spacemarks, are unable to read themselves), the past begins to accumulate, and its stages constitute reckoning levels for estimates of amount of change. And the present, now conscious of its comparative status, becomes for the first time specific *novelty.* In other words, novelty itself can exist, for our awareness, only in contrast with a past whose memory or record is assumed stable. *The empirical statuses of change and nonchange are therefore identical;* they are co-present in the physical context itself. And whatever is relative in each is, like all relativities, relative to an absolute. Duration must undergird change, not alone in the eternal quality of ideal aims, but also in the factualities of physical nature and of human history. Take another look at history:

History is of event, is it not? ergo, of the changing: further, in history the human will, while recording, rejects much more than it records, the infinite mass of the nonmemorable. Yet the positive act of history-making, as we observed, is one of remembering and conserving. Here, and in the cult of the dead, man has done his puny best to take over functions of preserving value commonly attributed to the gods. Through these efforts there has come about a growth of art and science and technique, an accumulation of what I have ventured to call "the Unlosables" [9]—cultural gains holding through, not only from dynasty to dynasty but across borders from civilization to civilization. This accumulating mass of cultural capital is destined—unless the race destroys itself—to bring to an end the frustrating rhythm of rise and decay of civilizations.

In man's solicitude for the passing, the shape of history is thus permanently altered; as far as any truth is durable, or any art, a durable base is provided—I will not say for "progress"—for that, too—but also for something far more significant, the maturing self-judgment of per-

[9] W. E. Hocking, *The Coming World Civilization,* Study III, "The Structure of History."

sons and eras, a dimension in depth of human self-consciousness—no slight achievement! The historical record itself, as a potential corporate memory-repertoire far exceeding any actual mind's capacity, is prized only on the condition that it may conceive *itself* to be factually everlasting! History, recording the transitory, *is a permanence* interior to change.

With all the signal success of this persistent purpose, this will to make human treasure into a growing treasury, we must yet recognize that *more passes than can possibly be conserved*—infinitely more. The philosophy of flux, however incomplete as a metaphysic, still presents a formidable obstacle to the notion of personal survival. With a just and terrible realism, it sheds its cold light on the immeasurable scope of forgetfulness: quite apart from catastrophe and loss, quakes, burnings, bombardments, there is the quiet but far more lethal activity of *selection* of what is keepable, in view of the finite capacity, not of record-warehousing, but of human caring. We shall eventually destroy the old letters, most of them, even with tears. For humanity can live in the present, and move into the future only at the cost of discarding, and with the appalling right, which is half a duty, to forget.

Is there, then, any deeper law of conservation? If among things we regard inanimate there is the scrupulous quantitative conserving of energy or momentum or mass, or of some function allied to these, which Galileo first recognized in his experiments with falling bodies as a certain inner veracity of nature, is the world less careful of its animate ingredients? Men have long believed in a certain natural legalism of conscious continuities whereby deeds have their unending effectiveness, whether by way of some law of Karma, or of the inner dynamics of durable social groups. Whitehead speaks of an "objective immortality" within the historical context, whereby each passing occasion, each personal life, contributes selective imprints to successive occasions.[10] Yet here again, the selective activity of "prehension" carries all the contingency of attention, interest, memory. The fundamental "intuition of permanence in fluency and of fluency in permanence," [11] in its abstract form, continues to demand satisfaction, as if there were in the nature of things some ultimate right not to perish utterly nor to be lost as a diminishing ripple in an endless sea. It persists as a question; and it is our question.

It penetrates to the inmost issue of metaphysics, why any caring or carers exist; and why—if there is a reason as well as a blind cause for their existing—they should perish, and how utterly they perish. There remains the possibility that the human will to conserve, partially potent within history, may be a symbol of an ultimate conserving power, supplementing the tragic fragmentariness of the human achievement, lawful and scrupulous toward personal quality as nature is lawful and scrupulous to its reservoir of fact.

The third and most formidable obstacle, that of the flux philosophy, so deeply grounded in truth, thus aids us in the definition of our final issue. We proceed to the metaphysical analysis.

[10] *Process and Reality,* pp. 527, 532 f.
[11] *Ibid.,* p. 526.

PART V

THE RELATIVITY
OF DEATH[1]

---

[1] Title of the Foerster Lecture on Immortality, Berkeley, California, January, 1942. This lecture was in two parts: i, Is Immortality Desirable?; ii, Is Immortality Possible? The first part has been here dealt with in Parts I–III of this book. The second part is expanded to the discussion now following. Its technical kernel, as originally stated, now appears in pages 220–234. Its original form first appeared, December 4, 1941, in *Journal of Philosophy* under the title, "Theses Establishing an Idealistic Metaphysics by a New Route."

PERSPECTIVE

THERE lies before us a direct attack upon our final issue, Is personal survival of death possible?

We shall take the term "personal" literally, meaning continuous identity of self-awareness, with elements of memory, questioning, and purpose. This implies that we shall not be discussing the possibility of *vicarious survival*, often put forward as a substitute for self-survival. Survival by transmission—the picking up by others of the impetus, the causes, the achievements of the life that passes—this survival-*in-aliis* presents no problem: it is the obvious vital absorbing-function of every continuing society. It is equally vital to each individual's outlook: each one, without conscious effort, lives in his forward time vista, anticipating his own effect as permeating an indefinite future. Reflection might show him that this effect has no limit in time: the ripples he may have made, though swiftly tending to unidentifiable diffusion, have their own immortality of momentum. The seven seas, in all truth, *must heed* each pebble cast! And to recognize the instant receptivity by ongoing life of one's own value attainment enhances the sense of worth held by the passing life. Even as one dies, he has in this prospect already lived forever! The genuine conservation of value herein implied is not to be minimized. Only, as vicarious, this objective immortality misses the kernel of our present concern, the *continuing subjectivity* of the individual self.

Let me also note that we are not speaking of the possible survival of a "soul," as distinct from the perishing body. This body disappears beyond recovery; and with it all power of communication through present effect with the existing assemblage of human associates. Yet, without bodiliness of some sort there can be no personal living. Existence, for a person, implies awareness of events in time—a continuity of particulars, not an absorption in universals or in The One. It is this particularity and temporalness that now concern us. And clearly, it is this concrete concern that creates our most radical impasse, our most spontaneous reading of the facts as implying extinction.

For in the human lot, just in proportion as it claims its belonging within *time*, there is an intrinsic perishing inseparable from time we are claiming as our own; and in death, the perishing runs deep, a lifetime is most definitely ended. It is true, the perishing is not absolute: it is precisely the physical that has *not* perished—the chemical and dynamic equations retain their integrity. Dust has remained dust, but also energy has remained energy. What has perished is the livingness of structure and function, the organic and personal integration of the persisting elements. Our question relates to *this* perishing, whether it is absolute, cutting through every strand of personal being—most vulnerable through its very marvel of unified complexity; or whether it, too, may be relative, leaving a germinal strand of selfhood intact. It is in this sense that I shall inquire into the possible *relativity of death*.

And if, as I do, we affirm this possibility, it will not be sufficient to find *that* survival is possible; we shall have at least to indicate *how* it is possible. Our question is Kantian in form, though Kant, who asked "How is experience possible?" failed, for reasons we shall consider, to ask "How is immortality possible?" This must be *our* question. The burden of the inquiry is heavy. And all the more so because, for many a serious thinker, the question as thus posed oversteps the borders of discretion, or perhaps of decent regard for the ultimate mysteries of being.

We owe to this attitude of respect for the world's reticence a word of recognition.

I

THE RIGHTS OF MYSTERY
AND INTUITION

I surmise that most of those who today hold a strong conviction of survival do so on the basis of intuition, without presuming to question how survival is possible. Long ago, a scientifically disposed colleague of mine wrote me as follows: "Since her [his wife's] death I have had a very simple faith that somehow her existence is not closed. There is a 'more' and she inhabits it: this seems to me too certain to be shaken by pure reason. I find reason groping blindly after experience, these days . . . I have felt too deeply to be discouraged any longer by mere logic. . . ." "Experience" was his word, implying direct perception. The Polish philosopher, Wincenty Lutoslawski, cited by William James in *The Energies of Men*, frequently averred in letters to me that immortality was for him a matter of immediate assurance; he was accustomed to inquire of others whether they, too, enjoyed this certitude—as a measure of their intuitive insight, prior to all argument.

To many, argument is rejected as a matter of principle: the mystery attending survival has its own signifi-

190

cance. The "veil" is beneficent: what is hidden is hidden for our good. And as they feel it, there is a certain philosophical crudity—perhaps an aesthetic and moral crudity as well—in attemping to see behind the curtain which God and Nature have established. Thus Elizabeth Barrett Browning, definite in her belief, is also definite in discouraging both investigation and complaint:

> Methinks we do as fretful children do,
> Leaning their faces on the window pane,
> To sigh the glass dim with their own breath's stain
> And shut the sky and landscape from their view.
>   And thus, alas, since God the maker drew
>   A mystic separation 'twixt those twain—
>   The life beyond us and our souls in pain,—
>   We miss the prospect we are called unto. . . .

Kant himself believed in this separation, though on a different ground. He refrained from asking How is immortality possible? because metaphysics, in his view, cannot be a scientific enterprise: immortality is not a matter of knowledge but of moral necessity—a "postulate." The moral imperative calls on us to become perfect in wish as well as in deed; and since we need endless time for this perfection, we must postulate the required continuance unless we are to believe the moral summons futile. In a kindred vein, Josiah Royce regarded survival as a matter neither of scientific evidence nor of wish but of a sobering moral demand: we must fulfill our unfinished task, that of achieving the individuality we here aspire to. He repeats, with a certain deprecation, his disavowal of knowledge-how: "I know not in the least, I pretend not to guess, by what processes this individuality of our human life is further expressed, whether through many tribulations as

here, or whether by a more direct road to individual fulfillment and peace. . . ." [1] He knows only that our individual being must find fulfillment: "further into the occult
it is not the business of philosophy to go." The word
"occult" carries here a touch of reproach.

In brief, for all that strand of philosophy which, after
Kant, has limited our metaphysical knowledge to the demands of duty, the survival of death is something that
ought to be: and for them, "this is all we know, and all we
need to know." Indeed, Kant, Fichte, and Lotze would
have hesitated to use the term "knowledge" in this context: to them the sense of duty is *sui generis*, a source of
affirmation distinct from and prior to knowledge.

I point out, however, that survival is a very empirical
issue for the survivor, and therefore for us who consider
it: difficult though the evidence may be, we cannot exclude truth-judgment from metaphysics. Duty itself has
its empirical assumptions; its demand is not issued from
a vacuum. For note:

"Duty" is *owed*; it is owed to someone who has a
"right." It can never be solitary, even while it may be
exceedingly lonesome! The painstaking care with which
an artist-workman insists on finishing his piece may be—
I surmise must be—self-imposed: "I am the only one," he
might say to himself, "who can judge when this job is
done." Nevertheless, his standard of judgment, strictly
his own, is the reverse of solitary. It is, like Emily Dickin-
son's lonely work, an appeal from available-and-fallible
judgments to a valid judgment, not here-and-now avail-
ble, but not a mere postulate. That standard, quite as
much as the explorative scientist's truth, is universal: like

[1] *The Conception of Immortality*, p. 80.

the scientist, the artist knows the world of his labors to be *a common world*; when he works for himself, he works for mankind—mankind at some future time judging truly. In this felt universality, as in Kepler's assurance of corroboration "whether by contemporaries or by posterity I care not," there is an implicit companionship. To this companionship, the omnipresent Thou-factor in all experience, *duty*, I say, *is a response*. The attempt to make duty an original source of affirmation is courageous, but it is an inversion of the actual order: there is first something we *know*—a being to whom duty is due—and then something we *ought*.[2]

With this perception, coming to clear light in our own century, *metaphysics at once becomes empirical*, a matter of experience in its primary assertions. The "veil" becomes in a measure understood: our aboriginal knowledge of the "real," with which we have always to do, is *habitually subliminal not because remote but because constantly present*. The type of knowledge Bergson and Whitehead call "intuitive" is the occasional voice of this persistent and unobtrusive awareness. With the recognition of its character, there may well be to some extent a lifting of the prohibition, resting so heavily both on our own sentiment and on the Kantian vein in philosophy, the veto of cognitive light on the issue of survival.

I feel strongly the ultimate right of mystery in the provisions of world structure. Gabriel Marcel has performed a clarifying service in adopting the term "mystery" for a type of issue in which, the inquiring self becomes part of the datum for its own inquiry, distin-

[2] "The moral will (is) the offspring of the ontological awareness. It is not loyalty that begets love; it is love that begets loyalty . . . love . . . and beauty are discoveries not postulates: we cannot seek them, we find them." *Jl. Phil.*, Feb. 2, 1956, p. 64.

guishing it from the term "problem" which indicates a challenge to the ingenuities appropriate to science and technology: such ingenuity has no part in the issues of death and continued life. One must move here with a certain awe, as between two perils, that of rationalizing what outpasses our instruments of analysis, and that of surrendering to the irrational—surrendering inquiries which belong to the responsibilities of thought. *Intuition is not irrational*; if it is valid at all, it contains an invitation to think—it has its rendezvous with reason, and must make its welcome good in the fullest light we can otherwise bring to bear as to the destiny of the soul.

*   *   *

To what extent, then, is intuition authoritative?

If, in contrast to Bergson, we insist that intuition is a knowledge not averse to conceptual interpretation, but requiring to be thought into a unity with the rest of our knowledge, shall not this conceptual expression have the last word? What shall we think of a philosopher who, after careful analysis, falls back on intuition for his final evidence? No one has dealt with the problem of immortality with more impressive technical care than Whitehead; yet when he has fully presented his case, and then raises the question, "What is the evidence . . . ?" he declares that "the only answer is the reaction of our own nature to the general aspect of life in the Universe," [3] i.e., to the common intuition of mankind. He concludes the discussion with an emphatic repudiation of primary reliance on analysis: "Logic, conceived as an adequate analysis of the advance of thought, is a fake. It is a superb instrument,

[3] Schilpp, *op. cit.*, p. 698.

but it requires a background of common sense," [4] and
common sense, I presume, is intuitive.

How are we to understand this—paradoxical but characteristic and refreshing—final appeal of the great logician to the authority of intuition? I take it as a matter
of simple epistemological wisdom. The hope for that sen-
sitiveness in truth-seeking which alone can reach the next
stage of insight in this matter lies in the unproved conviction that *ultimate issues have a simple handle*; and that
this simple handle remains through our thinking as a
guide, and finally as a test of validity. It belongs to the
justice of the world—and to the brotherhood of the race
—that whatever has significance for living comes within
the conspectus of the plain man, as intuition. Intuition, as
persistent awareness of, and reaction to, the real, is our
most directly empirical relation to the world, the most
universal, the most unrelenting. It precedes our analytical thinking, but also recurs after it with the authoritative query, "How far can your thought do justice to *me*?"

The authority is thus mutual! Without intuition,
thought is pallid; without thought intuition is ambiguous.
Accepting first-aid of imagination, intuition offers
through myth and proverb conflicting versions of its own
meaning: what it truly means can only be determined by
thought. Not, therefore, in despite of mystery, not in defiance of the established veil, but on behalf of veracity of
the race's vision of life's supplement, we must take the risk
of such rigorous conceptual analysis as we can bring to
bear on our issue.

4 *Ibid.*, p. 700.

II

THE ELEMENTAL CERTITUDES

How shall analysis begin?

If there were any relevant *a priori* certitudes available, they might be of use to us, provided that they were at the same time concrete—in Kant's terms, synthetic *a priori* judgments. We need not enter this contested territory if we observe that a beginning may be found *in experience*, allowing that experience, in the form of intuition, may have its own universal and indubitable character.

Western thought in dealing with survival has instinctively adopted this second course. It has not based itself, nor can we, upon a direct and personal intuition like that of Lutoslawski, an immediate assurance of his own immortality, even though regarded—as commonly in the Orient—as available to every enlightened and disciplined man. Western philosophers have sought a relevant intuition which without prior discipline could command universal consent. They have appealed to immediate self-awareness to verify a character of "the soul" from which it can be inferred either that the soul cannot survive, or that it must survive. They have undertaken to establish in this way the *that* of survival, pro or con. As for the *how* of survival, they have commonly fallen back on current myth.

Plato perfectly illustrates this procedure. In his most frequently quoted analysis he argues from the intuition that the soul is one, simple and indivisible—and the truism that the perfectly simple cannot be disintegrated—to the conclusion that the soul cannot die. As to the mode of survival, he offers the myth of Er and other engaging symbols—fully recognizing their mythical character— involving a journey to, and sojourn in, the Underworld, with an eventual return of many souls to life on earth in a new setting. The soul of the philosopher, however, "departs to the invisible world, and forever dwells, as they say of the initiated, in company with the gods." [1]

I suggest that we note first the intuitions which, in Western philosophy, have been dominantly appealed to in this connection; they will lead us to an alternative starting point in experience. We shall then turn to the imaginative supplements which have been used to indicate the how of survival, a matter far less attended to by philosophical discussion, one might fairly say neglected, and yet essential to our own inquiry.

Let me first come to the aid of Plato's repute in this matter, since he has been unjustly accused of beginning with an abstraction claiming to be an axiom. Kant deals hardly with the argument just quoted on the ground that it is a bit of "rationalist psychology" posing as metaphysics, a "paralogism." The statement that the soul is simple cannot be a report of experience, he declares, since if anything were purely simple it could in no wise present

[1] *Phaedo*, 80. Of the Platonic Socrates, the easy transition from dialectical literalness to current metaphor is part of his fascination: he assumes that his audience will understand his figures figuratively: witness his noble prayer to "Pan, and all ye other gods that haunt this place. . . ."

itself to us in experience.[2] If the simple excluded all complexity, Kant might be right; but that there is a unitary and identical element in experience, however complex, namely, the omnipresent I-think as a point of reference for all experience, empirical as well as logical and "transcendental," no one affirms more vigorously than Kant. On Kant's own ground, we must, I think, acquit Plato of the charge of beginning with a rational abstraction. And equally, upon the ground of our own experience, the final court of appeal:

For if we *care* for our own continued identity—a universal interest, implied in our search, as well as in every impulse of "self-preservation"—it would indeed be odd if we cared for the continuance of something of which we *have no experience*! To love life, and to love "*my being alive*," are not two things, but one. It is doubtful whether to "love life" means anything other than to love living. And to love living is to love a continuing experience of identity, in the subjective reference of successive items of awareness.

Change itself, to be known as change, must register itself upon an unchanging subject. Experiencing as a continuing process steadily distinguishes this enduring selfhood from the multiple and shifting contents composing the "stream of consciousness," or that "bundle of perceptions in continual flux and movement" offered by Hume as the only discoverable selfhood. We need these "contents," but we are not they; they are ours. And with this distinction, at once analytic and empirical, we *perceive*

[2] Kant is verbally criticizing a Cartesian form of the Platonic premiss, namely, that the soul "is a simple substance"—a form which Plato obviously did not use; and which Kant does not need in his refutation. His point is, that "*das Einfache in ganz und gar keiner Erfahrung vorkommen kann.*" K.d.r.V., p. 588.

some sort of self-durability. What sort, and how lasting, is not part of the *datum.* But without following Plato's radical inference, we recognize the pertinence of his clue. And without joining Lutoslawski, we catch sight of what he meant! To put it in cautious terms of modern analysis, the position of the *subject*, in all experiencing, is ontologically distinguishable from that of the *objects* entertained.

When Descartes, basing himself on this same intuition, added the notion of "substance," he thought to introduce a further barrier to annihilation in death. At the same time, he introduced a further problem into his philosophy. Substance being defined as self-sufficient being, dependent on nothing else, must be indestructible. The soul, he says in almost verbal agreement with Augustine, is an unextended, immaterial substance, simple, indivisible—hence imperishable: its essence is the I-think. Its power to survive, on this showing, depends not on its verifiable simplicity, but on a substantial imperviousness which outpasses the reach of intuition. Likewise the monads, as of Leibniz and personalists, McTaggart, Howison, and others. The monads, as noncommunicating globules of being, like Platonic souls, eternally pre-exist as well as perdure. Each such entity, containing its own version of the entire world, should be able to be directly aware of its own perpetuity, unborn and indestructible. But in so far as the monad notion outpasses intuition, and prescribes an inescapable identity through all past time, it collides with other intuitions. Those who, like myself, believe that they have been born of two parents, a belief supporting a memory intuition of limited pastness, implying a definite beginning and a finite past history, are debarred from sharing this confidence in inherent two-way eternity. And there is this material difficulty, that if with a Pythagoras or a Luto-slawski one considers that he retains actual memories of pre-vious embodied existences, he must be prepared to set aside with a firm hand the impressive phenomena of heredity!

For our own analysis, I propose to adhere to intuition as a starting point, but to a different intuition. I suggest a phase of experience whose certitude, if not explicitly universal, is yet capable of being brought to universal affirmation. I call attention to our self-awareness, not as simple, not as substantial, not as monadic, but as *free—* free in a sense to be carefully defined.

None of the thinkers above referred to was wrong in the direction of his search—self-awareness is the nucleus of metaphysical experience. Their defect has been that their metaphysic was too little empirical: it requires the revi-sion which the present century has given to the Cartesian "I think, I exist." What we now recognize is that this *nuclear certitude is composite*: in our lonely self-aware-ness we are not and cannot be solitary; the thinker with-out something-thought-about is a zero; and the something-thought-about is something-to-be-shared, as common object, with a "Thou," co-present with the self. With this triadic character of nuclear experience, the I-It-Thou inseparable, the self-sufficient monadic outline is de-stroyed; and immortality of the ego-by-itself ceases to be plausible, still less axiomatic.

The certitude we seek will be found not in the self-en-closed ego, but in the *active relation of the self to its world of common objects*, fully accepted as essential to its own being. As experience acquires, for the self, an objec-tive character, as shared with a Thou, there is insepara-bly an objectivity in the sphere of its action. Activity is aboriginal and impulsive; but as impulsive action affects a common world, the power to act becomes a *power to effect change* in this world-not-myself; and if the change is durable, the power to act is *ipso facto power to create.* If the power to create is an outcome of a power-to-choose in creation, the self·is exercising what is generally called "freedom," meaning here freedom in the metaphysical sense of power to originate concrete fact. In my judgment the exercise of this power is a factor in all self-conscious being: *we act knowing this freedom,* whether or not we single it out for explicit assertion.

Let us now observe the pertinence of this certitude-of-concrete-freedom to our inquiry regarding survival.

*   *   *

Freedom is inseparable from our self-awareness as able-to-act, even prior to our engagement with outer fact. Our most aboriginal freedom is exercised in choosing between *effort and rest*; and especially in regard to one type of effort, the effort of thinking. With the subject matter offered in sensation I may deal passively (or aesthetically) as a sensing entity; or I may deal with it actively as a thinking entity. Were it not for this alternative, this freedom, there could be no touch of duty in the call actually there, and mingling inseparably with what one's own life impulse dictates—the call *not merely to sense but to think* this mutual stuff, and thereby transform *sensa* into object things and events, materials for a common world, ultimately for a common science. This effort of thought is the first field of duty; and freedom is presupposed—it is, in this sense, prior to duty.

Freedom thus prepares its own further stage, that of acting within and upon a world having the objectivity of structure revealed by this our thinking. It is here that *imagination is brought into play,* as shaping the course of our creative action; and imagination itself receives in this interplay a quality of *actual possibility*, linking it with the reality of the objective order.

To be free, therefore, is to be, by way of our individual imagination, in possible command of the course of nature. What is going to happen is, at some point, that which I will to happen—I, and *not nature*! For nature does not imagine. If, therefore, in our power to create, we are in a position, however narrow and perilous, to dictate the happening of nature, there is in our being something outside of nature. And what is outside of nature, in relation of *control*, is not at that point at the mercy of perishings within nature.

If, then, we accept this intuition of concrete freedom as among our elemental certitudes, we have a promising basis—the only promising basis so far as we have seen—for analytic examination of the judgment that survival is possible. For my part I accept this intuition of freedom as valid. Its statement and purport are indeed matters of philosophical contention through the ages; the skeptical reflections that incline us ever and anon to a view of external determination pervading all our seemingly free choices are achievements of the sophisticated mind—importations from world views of vast dignity and importance, but subsequent: I shall not here broach this issue.[3]

I note simply that if the experience of freedom offers light upon the *that* of survival, the *how* of freedom might do as much for the how of survival. Kant gives no answer to this question; for him, freedom is a postulate, and further, his view of freedom is not in our sense concrete.

Let us now turn, as above proposed, to the imaginative supplements dealing with the current conceptions of how survival is possible.

[3] The later analysis of freedom will dispose of it. Page 230 below.

III

FROM IMAGINATION TO PHILOSOPHY

THE question, how survival is possible, which impedes free access to the *that*, has, as we have noted, been commonly left by philosophers and public alike to mystery and symbol. Their language, alike in myth and tradition, is largely the language of imagination: "In my Father's house are many mansions. . . . I go to prepare a place for you. . . ."

This willing relinquishment of literality has its good reasons: among others, the swift access of current symbol to the truth of feeling.[1] Socrates in the moment of death reverted to the imagery of Greek tradition—"Crito, I owe a cock to Asklepios": the categorical knowledge he needed included no chart of his impending passage; it was simply a *that*, namely "that nothing evil can befall a good man, whether in life or in death." Still, the language of imagination is not a pure evasion: it is translatable; it has its

[1] I know no more eloquent witness to this than the "folk-sermons" brought together by James Welldon Johnson under the title *God's Trombones*, especially the funeral sermon, "Go Down Death," neither speaker nor hearer deluded by the imagery that carries as no literality could do the realities of emotion.

unwritten responsibilities to objective truth. No doubt, imagination is a playground—its other name is fancy, privileged in its mission of release to a degree of insouciance. Yet complete irresponsibility is an unattainable ideal; even the fairiest of fairy tales must retain a wraith of verisimilitude—the beanstalk that sustains the exploits of Jack, the Giant Killer, must have remote analogies in the world of vegetation!

We must assume this residual will-to-veracity as lurking within the vast assemblage of imagery relating to survival. He would be brave, indeed, who should venture to plot on a cosmic chart the various abodes of the dead, their occupations in the other world, the modes of their arrival thither, the forms of judgment that determine their lot. Is there a modicum of metaphysical insight giving continued vitality, through ages of increasing scientific sophistication, to the play of poetic and prophetic imagery in this field?

I once thought, and have said, that it is easier for us moderns to imagine another life than to believe it.

I had in mind not alone the common literary appeal, deliberately allegorical, as in Sartre's *Les Jeux sont Faits,* or in Santayana's *Dialogues in Limbo*; or with more serious purpose, as in James B. Pratt's portrayal of the embarrassment of "Professor Materialist" who, knowing himself to have been killed, is confronted with the dismaying evidence of his own survival.[2] I had in mind, as well, the wholly serious efforts of religious thought to give substance, for the apprehension of critical contemporaries, to the conception of another world. As we leave the realm of poetry, are we to keep what seems essential to

[2] *Adventures in Philosophy and Religion,* p. 215.

life in this world—a continuity of memory, a time sequence, a sphere of action, a persistence of achieved
knowledge, love, purpose, question-and-answer? Hard to
believe? Yes. But easy to imagine? I thought so; I now
doubt it.

Easy, only so long as fanciful imagination keeps critical imagination in abeyance. There is a *responsible imagination* which, while allowing fanciful imagination free
play in symbolizing the unknown, still retains in reserve
its own functions of exploration and criticism. It is well
to recognize that the principal agent in bringing errant
imagination into the area of truth is *also imagination*, an
imagination tamed by the demands of realism, but none
the less imagination. At every step forward we rely on a
valid imagination: if we fancy the ice thick when it is
thin, we may need to revise the set of signs by which our
imaginative forecast is guided. It is through imagination,
in the field of science, that poor hypotheses are replaced
by better, and unworkable inventions by inventions that
will work. The Copernican Revolution had first to be a
feat of imagination; the Einsteinian Relativity a further
feat of the same order. How else than through imagination, inventive while disciplined, are we to reach the
hypothesis that will finally be verified? Thinking *is* directed imagining.[3]

[3] Where physical theory leads, as today, to conceptions whose elements are no longer modelable, imagination has to forego reliance upon
its most available building stuff, the visual image. The advance of
thought has still to use symbols as the elements of its equations; and
for these symbols there is what I would suggest calling a subsensuous
imagining. We have to recall that not all experience is limited to the
"five senses," nor to the larger number we now recognize. In our own
sense of life, the "coenesthesia" which is neither visual, auditory, nor
tactual, we have an element of the wider empiricism capable of noting
the *élan vital* of natural event. The continuing fertility of scientific

We must therefore revise the thesis that it is easier to imagine survival than to believe it. This is true of irresponsible imagination; belief in its products is inhibited by imagination itself. But responsible imagining is our key to the structure of the world; and for our defective thesis we may substitute this one: *Whatever we can responsibly imagine is structurally possible* in the given universe.

I propose, therefore, that we submit our free imaginings of another world, as scene of another life, and of the passage thereto, to the test of a critical imagining which may reveal what structure in the universe could permit the passage, or show the nature of the hinge between one life and another. Let us attempt a transition from the popular way of using imagination in regard to survival, to the element of responsible metaphysic therein contained.[4]

*   *   *

Irresponsible imagining, presenting life after death on the available patterns of present experience, with due modifications for the advance of meaning, has commonly dealt easily with the question of passage. Making full use of the license of myth, it has fancied that we pass from one life to another as we pass from region to region in this sphere: there is a *journey of the soul* from this world to its next abode.

Generally speaking, in our own traditions, Heaven is

hypothesis depends more than ever on a quasi-mystical sympathy with the intangible processes of nature: visual imagining must be supplemented by vital imagining, none the less explorative.

[4] With the encouragement of Kant's *"Uebergang von der gemeinen sittlichen Vernunfterkenntnis zur philosophischen"*, in Metaphysics of Morals, 1785.

"above" and Hell "beneath"; but a "Western Paradise" is a natural suggestion of the setting sun; and the Egyptian conception of a voyage with the sun in his underworldly excursion has a kindred root. Responsible imagining has been slow to intrude upon legitimate poesy the consideration *that whatever can be reached by a journey is in this space*, not in another space. Or generalizing, whatever situation can be reached by spatial transition is in this world, and not another, when "world" is identified with the given system of events in the total space-time universe. If we are to think in tenable terms of another life in an other world, we must employ some other than spatial transition for the passage. The consideration is obvious, yet so tenacious is the spatial image that all the revelations of Copernican and post-Copernican cosmology have not banished the query whether some other suns may have planets that could serve as the scene of life for surviving souls.

Giordano Bruno, having lighted on the valid notion of endlessness of the cosmos, and having written that "there are numberless particular worlds similar to this of the earth," speculated that in view of the divine goodness they, or some of them, were presumably abodes of life: the moon seemed to him one of the most likely. And when Galileo found, as he thought, mountains and seas there, the probability appeared to mount toward certitude; and the query was not slow to arise whether some of these were providing homes for spirits of our departed. The advance of astronomy has dealt unkindly with this companionable outlook into sidereal spaces.[5] But the central

[5] Sir James Jeans, in November, 1941, lectured at the Royal Institution on "Is There Life on the Other Worlds?" in which he referred to Bruno's speculation purely on the physical side. After showing that

difficulty is that no such exploration of the universe has any bearing whatever on "another world" for the careers of departed souls. The hinge of transition is *not a spatial hinge*: it is not a journey, nor a passage from compartment to compartment, nor a concealment as "When you and I behind the veil are passed," nor is it the crossing of a stream, whether Jordan or the Styx. All such figures have their pertinence; yet all of them tend to distract us, if I am not mistaken, from the essential simplicity and inwardness of the event.

But there are other conceptions of the transition, from which the spatial image is dropped. While Dante's journey to the underworld is spatial, almost geographical, aided indeed by "a certain drowsiness," John Bunyan's transition, equally artful, is of another type: "As I walked through the wilderness of this world, I lighted on a certain place where was a den, and laid me down in that place to sleep; and as I slept, I dreamed a dream." It is true that the dream is itself of a journey, terminating in "the Heavenly City"; but Bunyan's personal transition from waking to dreaming, and from dreaming to waking ("So I awoke, and behold, it was a dream") is not

---

nothing within the solar system would answer as an abode for such life as ours, he used the calculus of probability to reach the judgment that perhaps two million million suns are provided with planets, that an appreciable number of these have conditions resembling those of our earth, atomic constitution being approximately the same, and inorganic compounds familiar to us presumably prevalent. As for the organic compounds, the crucial item in this case, for whose probability we have and can have no computing basis until we know more of the conditions of their origin, Sir James rightly found no data. (I believe it can be shown that this probability is of the order of one over an infinitude of the class of aleph sub-zero, a very "vanishing" quantity indeed.) *Science*, June 12, 1942.

a journey. The dream world is not "somewhere" in the waking world: there is no road of passage, nor any astronomical line of distance and direction, between London or Bedford gaol and the Heavenly City. The passage between them is as swift as a change in the direction of thought. Bunyan himself, absorbed in the career of his pilgrim, might as swiftly have been "brought to earth" by an interruption. I raise the question whether we have not here something not identical with, but more literally than the journey image akin to, a believable "hinge of transition" between this world and another.

This proposal would relieve us at once of a burden of imported and impossible physical interpretation; it does so, however, at the cost of suggesting that the other-world may be, like all things reachable by a mere turn of attention, such stuff as dreams are made on—subjective, insubstantial, less than actual. Our critical imagination hesitates to adopt the dream transition as more than a possible analogy. Any life beyond death that could concern us must be at least as actual as the present life: it could, according to some conceptions, be more so, as a state of being to which one "awakens from the dream of life."

Remarking only that even so, the transition would be mental, I regard the objection as of the essence. It opens the entire issue as to the relation between the "mental" and the "real." We have here to deal with the convinced monism of our scientific era: there is but one real universe, one space-time-event context, one world of nature. The word "other" always means a relation between objects *within* this universe: the given space includes all the space there is—hence there is no outside, no "other," perhaps

no totality from which another universe could stand
apart! To this physical monism, and all it implies, we
must give full attention: I shall later call to mind Minkowski's Memoir of 1908, in which he vigorously assaulted
the doctrine of monism (though chiefly for purposes of
calculation), making the radical assertion that "from
henceforth we shall speak no more of Space and Time,
but of spaces and times." [6] For the present, let me say
only this:

In so far as an imagined or dreamed experience does,
under any circumstances, approximate actuality, the
transition between present experience and that experience
reveals a structural possibility of the universe, significant
for the event of death. And I point out that there *is* a
phase of experience in which the imagined does approximate the actual, and hold responsible relation to it, while
remaining literally "other." In the genuine and incessant
experience of deliberation leading to free decision, we are,
prior to the decision, in presence of two worlds—the actual world before us, and the world of our imagined future action. This world of contemplated action (which
we hold ourselves free to cancel, until the commitment of
decision is made) differs from dream as *not totally unreal*:
it has the partial reality implied in *genuine "possibility."*
Could we give a true account of this situation—and we
shall duly undertake it—we should be on the way to a
philosophical conception of the possibility of survival.

As a prior step in this direction, let me call attention
to a somewhat neglected phase of our imagining—the
way in which, while imagining events and deeds, we
imagine our *own persons* as engaged in these imagined
contexts.

[6] Below, page 224 n.

IV

DOUBLE ROLES
OF SELF AND WORLD

In our ordinary meditations about the world of science and of history, we naturally leave ourselves out of the picture: the way of objective truth is, for the most part, to forget ourselves. Yet the knowledge does not forsake us that we are, in fact, a part of the world envisaged by both science and history; and if reminded of this circumstance, we can easily find ourselves pursuing the double role of self-observing and self-observed.

When the observed self is considered by the observing self as set in his natural surroundings, or as acting there, this observing self would as a rule entirely accept for the observed self the judgment, "The self is in the world, not the world in the self." This was the position of Alfred Whitehead in 1925, when in his *Science and the Modern World* he wrote that "we are *within* a world of colours, sounds, and other sense objects. . . . We seem to be ourselves elements of this world in the same sense as are the other things which we perceive" (page 125, my italics). Yet when in 1934 he published two lectures given at Chicago on "Nature and Life" he made a supplement to this statement. He wrote of "a baffling antithetical relation" whereby, while the soul itself appears "as one of the components within the world," it is also true that "in one sense the world is in the soul." [1] How does he reach this second position? By becoming aware of *the observing self* —easily forgotten—who *entertains the vision of that world* in which the observed self is contained and surrounded. As the observed self, I am in the world. As the observing self, the world is in me. Yet I am the same self; and with this duality of position, the entire perspective of reality changes. Could it be the case that the self which is within the world, an object among objects, is not the entire self? Or could it be that the world contained within the observing self is not identical with the world which contains the observed self—two worlds, descriptively the same, ontologically different, held together by the intention of an identical self, assuming two roles in relation to its environment?

There are occasional experiences coming to everybody in which the self perceives itself as other, while still the same. They are not matters of mystery, but chiefly of emphasis—a self-separation which momentarily exaggerates the continuous function of self-awareness and self-judgment. We have seen how, in self-accusation, the judging self assumes a character different from the self that is judged. No one is a liar unless he knows that he is a liar, for it is not a lie to speak an untruth supposing it to be truth. Yet if the liar knows he is a liar, and confesses that he is a liar, he must be a truthteller in denouncing himself as liar. This, the ancient paradox of Epimenides, is no

---

[1] *Nature and Life,* p. 40. He calls this relation "mutual immanence," recognizing the topological self-contradiction as nevertheless somehow the case.

other than the constant and normal doubleness of a self that must live by standards of self-judgment.

If I now cite certain experiences of my own, essentially trivial, by way of illustrating these occasional exaggerations of normal doubleness which bear upon our discussion, I do so to recall to the reader similar experiences of his own, and to suggest their possible significance. One such, wholly commonplace, left on my mind for some time a curious impression, not that we can imagine survival but not believe it, but the obverse—that we can believe our own annihilation, but are wholly unable to imagine it. (For those who find these tales unimpressive or irrelevant, I simply ask that they be passed over: the argument does not depend on them.)

The time is 1892, more or less. The scene is the right-of-way of a single track railroad, between Aurora, Illinois, and Waukegan—the Elgin, Joliet, and Eastern Railroad, then a new belt line around Chicago. It is a summer day. A lone figure carrying a pot of white paint and a brush, stoops every 100 feet to cover a chalk mark on the inside of the rail with a vertical line of paint, and every 500 feet to paint a number. The crew of the civil engineering department are measuring the track of the railway for inventory purposes. The chalk markers, with the steel tape, have moved ahead of the painter, who doesn't mind being alone. He has become interested in the numbers.

He is, at this moment, in a cut. The banks rise on either side of him above his eye level; the breeze is shut off; the heat is oppressive. The only sounds are the humming of insects and the occasional nervous flutter of a disturbed grasshopper's wings. The painter is painting the number 1800. He is amused to note the possibility of putting this number series into one-to-one correspondence with the years of the century. He begins to supply the numbers with events, at first bits of history—Civil War and family background. This imaginary living-through-past-time becomes as real an experience as the rail-

painting, and far more exciting! 1865, 1870—suddenly 1873,
my birth year: "Hello! Hocking is here!" Every mark, from
now on, numbered or not, is entangled with personal history.
But very soon, 1892, *the present*: the painter's story and the
actual story coincide: I paint the Now! From this point, memory is dismissed; it gives place to anticipation, dream, conjecture—there is something relentless in the onmoving of these
numbers, to be filled with something—but with what? 1893—
will it be the new Chicago University? 1900—where shall I
be? 1950, fairly old, very likely gone. 1973, a hundred years
from birth—surely gone: "Good-by, Hocking!" I see myself
as dead, the nothingness of non-being sweeps over me. I have
been for four years an ardent disciple of Herbert Spencer, un-
happily but helplessly convinced that man is as the animals;
the race moves on, the individual perishes, the living something has become—nothing; "And not the pillow at your cheek
So Slumbereth." For the first time I realize, beyond the mere
clack of words, the blankness of annihilation. And no doubt,
just because of this swift sense of no-sense, the shock was
intense as I realized, with the same swiftness, that *it was I,
as surviving, who looked upon myself as dead,* that it had to
be so, and that because of this, annihilation can be spoken of,
but *never truly imagined.* This was not enough to free me
from the spell of Spencer, but it cracked that spell: the rest
of the day was spent in a new lightness of heart, as if I had
come upon a truth that was not to leave me. I was glad to
be alone.

Obviously, this situation was most artificially built: the
mechanical action of brush and paint must inevitably run past
the relived life and compel a sharp vision of the end, and
then of "the long, long time the world shall last." Yet the un-
fading impression left by this experience carries the question
whether this doubleness of self may not have a natural reality:
may not the observing self be enduring, while the observed
self drops away?

There are certain other experiences I might mention,
experiences which bring the observed and the observing
self more literally into juxtaposition. They were experi-

ences of seeming to observe oneself from the outside. Though they tend to attach themselves to this inquiry, I hesitate to recall them, inasmuch as, until recently, I had dismissed them as somewhat disoriented dreams: they were connected with an illness.

Some of my early years were spent on the Eastern Shore of Maryland, at Easton, Talbot County. Our family, unacclimated, suffered severely from malaria, then called "chills and fever" or "ague." I enjoyed long sieges of this malady, whose later stages were attended with vivid dreams some of which I have been unable to forget. Interspersed with these dreams was a recurrent experience which resembled them, but differed in two respects: it was definitely enjoyable, and its visual contents appeared to be actual. It seemed to me that I floated upward toward the ceiling, and looked down upon myself in bed. I was not at all impressed by the situation as absurd— it seemed quite natural that I should be mobile in independence of my official body, able to observe that body as with another pair of eyes, or perhaps more accurately as though one had no need of eyes in order to see!

(This oddity is, of course, not unusual; for in any dream with visual imagery, though one's eyes are closed, there is no impediment to vision: one sees, as it were, without eyes, or with dreamed eyes, and without raising any questions!)

These experiences, as I said, I had dismissed as insignificant. They were, however, to some extent revived, with a question mark, by the experience of a friend many years later, related to me with extreme care for accuracy of statement.

She, the wife of a colleague, had been at the crisis of pneumonia; her husband and the physician were at her bedside. She was presumed to be, if not in coma, at least unconscious of her surroundings. But she heard their conversation, which was not encouraging. The physician left the room, and shortly after, the husband also went out. She noted his movements; she wanted to go with him; she found herself free to move at will; she saw herself lying there; she followed her husband. He crossed the hall, closing the door, and went into his library. She saw him pace to and fro, then take down a book from a shelf, open it and gaze at the page without reading on. She saw the page. He put the book back, and returned to her bedside. She was there; she had not moved; she heard him plead with her, in the hope that his words might reach her consciousness, to try to come back to life. She was aware that it was in her power to make this effort; hard as it was, and unwelcome, she made it, for his sake. When she had recovered, she wished to test the apparent experience. When her husband was in the library, she took down the book she had seen him take, opened to the page, and asked him whether he had any recent memory of it. Much startled, he recounted the episode as she had seemed to see it.

Experiences of this sort can be of no importance to science; as unrepeatable and unverifiable, they are significant only to those who have known the like. But they suggest possibilities that concern us.

The function of unusual experience is, as a rule, not so much to answer questions as to open them. They stir us out of our habitual assumptions. They may illuminate; but the final answers must be in the common experiences of mankind—this has become my firm conviction. If there is any truth in "mystic experience," it is what every man subconsciously knows, and what thought can eventually validate.

The analogical experiences I have here recounted simply raise the question whether ordinary consciousness has *an inner plurality of perspective*—whether an "other life" in "another world" are not always "within you." Certainly, imagination and dream are always in operation; without them we take no step into the future. Dream in sleep is but imagination without the competing presence of the actual. In my judgment, while the content of such dreams has as a rule far less significance than psychoanalysis tends to read into it, *the structure of dream,* the possibility of a well-developed world which seems to happen to us even while we are—in part—creating it, is highly significant.

For our question, the meaning of imagination and dream is best seen in their shaping of action. In all deliberating and deciding, we employ them to prepare an alteration of the actual world. As deliberation passes into act, we see in operation one of the "hinges" of the world; what was a moment ago the other-world of fancy becomes, by the determination of our everyday freedom, a bit of objective history. The imagined linkages swing "down" into the linkages of fact. They *fit there* with a silent perfection of continuity.

I stand on our actual awareness of freedom to create change. Our knowledge of freedom implies awareness of our double posture in the universe: we are both creature and creator—our lives are an "*apprenticeship* in creativity." [2] As creatures we are "receptive" i.e., passive to an outer action: experience takes its name from the fact that it is "given" to us, and whatever gives us experience gives us therewith our being—our createdness is continual.[3] Hence we are not alone: our existence and our potential work are included within that objective purpose; and because of this inclusion, one's life effort may take shape as a "task," or as the Confucians say, one's *Ming,* one's Decree of Heaven. But this continual createdness does not cancel our other posture, that of being creators. The

[2] *Meaning of God,* pp. 153 f.

[3] Subjective idealism fails to ask how we can give ourselves to ourselves.

"task" itself is not piecework designed by the Master: its scope is to produce something which, *without our deed, the universe could not contain,* and for which the universe is—or should be—glad! God himself has not prethought your conception; your creation, within its bounds, is as real as his, and so your freedom.

If this is the implication of our freedom—and I present this view as an hypothesis for our consideration—the *meaning* of survival of death is given a new light. Our interest in continuance is not simply the fulfillment of duty, the completion of a preassigned task, as Kant and the voluntarists propose. Our concern is also *that the universe may do its duty by us*—allowing us, for example, to reach the answer to the questioning which our life contains, "to know as we are known." The "how" of survival will not be by the force of inescapable duty alone, but by our right as well, including our right to know the "Last Judgment" of the worth or lack of worth in what we have aspired to do. And also, understanding that judgment, to join in it, so that in the end we *stand self-judged*, not judged alone by an absolute Other.

It has long seemed to me the chief moral indictment of a broken-off existence—supposing death to be the absolute end, our being blanked out in the midst of an always unfinished labor—that the terminal judgment of one's work, one's lonely belief in that work at the moment of death, has for the dying one no sequel. Those who fall in battle shall never know whether they have died in vain. In a world that lets die, the faith of the doer remains at best a tragic question thrown out upon an unheeding Process of Nature—for with the best assurance, faith and work look forward, far forward—not for praise, but for truth. Must they stumble into the night? "Why has Thou forsaken me?"

This depth of yearning for valid judgment is far deeper than any hope for a rewarding justice, or any fear of a retributive justice, in unchanging heavens or hells. On the count of "justice" most souls should be in both places. For a while. But this more genuine need is, I believe, at the heart of the universal concern for survival, and of the intuition that it must be so.

And in the underlying and equally universal experience of power-to-create in freedom, a radical philosophical analysis, to which we now turn, should find instruction as to its possibility, and also as to the "how."

In this analysis, there will be much intentional repetition, i.e., themes already touched on will reappear, sustained and clarified by their systematic connections. Our concern now is with the connections.

V

THE PHILOSOPHICAL
ANALYSIS

DEFINITION: By "physical monism" I mean the doctrine that there is (and can be) only one world of physical nature.

For this view, the word "the"—in such phrases as "the world," "the universe," "the cosmos," all referring to the same totality—is decisive. It signifies that there is no other—that the system of entities and events in the space-time order now present to us is single and unique. This totality is unbounded (or "infinite") in the sense that there is nothing else of the same kind outside of it. The relation "outside of" refers to distinctions of position between elements of the system: entities or events within the system may be "outside of" one another. A continued exploration of outsideness or "externality" would thus forever remain within the system; the phrase "outside the system" would be meaningless.

Definition: By "concrete freedom" I mean the capacity, for human action, of deciding between genuine alternatives—genuine in the sense that any one of such alternatives is "possible," and can become part of the actual world of nature at the will of the decider.

i. Physical monism is inconsistent with concrete freedom.

Physical monism implies that all determinants of physical change are physical. As such, they are subject to quantitative measurement.[1] On this condition, given any total configuration of the system at any time and the laws of change, the configuration at any other time—before or after without limit—is, in general and in theory, determinable. If into this well-ordered system some "principle of indeterminacy" enters, such as formulated by Heisenberg for certain subatomic processes, it would still remain true that *no nonphysical factors are relevant to what emerges* from the ambiguous situation.

Concrete freedom, however, requires that a mental event, a "decision," itself original, can determine which of diverse physical alternatives shall become actual. Concrete freedom is therefore impossible unless physical monism is somewhere in error. Such error, I suggest, may lie in its assumption of the single-and-unique character of space. We examine (§§ ii. iii. iv) the credentials of that assumption.

ii. Kant's argument for Newtonian space-time monism.

[1] The words "physical" and "mental" as here used involve no ambiguity: I do not here define them, appealing to common usage. I point out, however, that their contrast assumes that what is physical, as "objective" and measurable, carries with it the elimination of the conscious subject *as physical factor*. If we refuse to recognize this distinction, and with Russell and Whitehead attempt an intramental (essentially subjective) definition of the physical object as a "family of perspectives," the cleanness of physics is sacrificed, and the metaphysical issues are obscured.

Kant's view of the cosmos, based on that of Newton, holds that there can be but one space order, infinite in extent, and one time order, also infinite; space and time being prior and independent conditions of all events within them. His view of freedom had to be consistent with a single and necessary system of physical events, including the behavior of the bodily organism. It could not be concrete freedom, as here defined.

But why has space, for Kant, no legitimate plural?

He calls to witness what we ourselves know and mean by space. If we speak of "spaces," we mean various parts or regions of the one space: if we try mentally to set another space outside of the given space, we merely define a distant area, and "distance" belongs wholly to the space we have. We are (he holds) really *unable to conceive* a literally-other space. And for this reason: that space is not a thing perceived but our way of perceiving, innate and inescapable: it is the mode of arrangement whereby the manifold data of sense are ordered—external to each other, and yet together in the same infinite room. It is, in short, the "form of external apprehension" not itself apprehended. We cannot see space nor touch it; but whatever is seen or touched is "there": space is, in Hegel's accurate phrase, a nonsensous sensibility, an *"unsinnliche Sinnlichkeit"*! Then, thinks Kant, the "thereness" must somehow precede the sensations, or at least be ready to spring to life as sensation begins—a necessary presupposition of experience.

And once on duty as the thereness of physical experience, it remains on duty, identical, forever. As valid for all such data, it can have no boundary. As endless, there is "no room" for any other: it *is* the "room." And it must be one and changeless through all time; for if it were alterable or withdrawable, what would become of our measures of *motion*, as fundamental to experience as our measures of extent? Apprehending experience as spatial can hardly be called an "act" of the self; for action is a deed-at-a-time, and our space-perceiving, so far as it is a deed at all, is one-for-all-time. Instead of mysteriously calling it a "timeless act," let us say that for Kant it is inseparable from self-conscious identity: to be *the same self* both here and there, and from day to day, is to relate things and events to each other by way of an identical and infinite space. And if there can be but one space, there can be but one world of nature: we are committed to physical monism.

iii. Kant's argument, already discounted by views of Leibniz, later challenged by non-Euclidean geometries.

The monads of Leibniz had, each one, its private mirror of the entire universe. The space and time of the unfolding world scene for each monad were, as in the Kantian world scene, infinite; there were therefore as many co-existing infinite spaces as there were monads. No monad could have been aware of this multiplicity, nor of the problem of interpenetration, since for each monad its own mirror world was the one, real, total, and unique world; and all the other monads were therein represented as sharing the single infinite space. It was only God, and Leibniz as author of the conception, who on Leibniz' own terms could be aware of the duplication of infinitudes, and he himself ought not to know of it! If Leibniz had meditated the problem how his monads, as unextended "metaphysical points," yet each a world for itself ("*un monde à part*"), could coexist as entertaining infinitudes without interaction, his answer might have been that we are not dealing with multiple spaces, but only with the thoughts of spaces, and that thoughts require no room at all—not even the thought of infinite space! The suggestion is significant, and bears on the issue not only of other spaces, but also of other worlds. But it escapes the difficulty only by denying that there is any such thing as a "real" space as contrasted with thought space—there are only private thought spaces. We do not accept this hypothesis; but we recognize that Leibniz' world picture disposes of Kant's doctrine that plural spaces are inconceivable. If Kant, for whom also space was not a thing-in-itself but a way of our apprehending, had asked himself whether different persons as different apprehenders not only might but must have different spaces, his certitude of the singleness of space might have been shaken.

In a quite different way, the development after Kant of non-Euclidean geometries has accustomed mathematicians to thinking of different *types* of space; and if there can be different kinds of space, then since any given space can be of only one kind, there can be different spaces. The geometers Bolyai, Lobatschewski, Riemann, and others, had no difficulty in contemplating them together, in their plurality; but they failed to investigate the relation between coexisting instances. To some extent, it is true of these non-Euclidean geometries that they were not considered as coexisting, but as alternatives of interpretation—various possible logical constructs of our actual physical experience.[2] Even so, their mutual exclu-

---

[2] So far as this is the case, the several types of space might more accurately be called so many *algebras* for expressing spatial experience, or in our common phrase, analytic geometries. I judge also that the "spaces" of which Minkowski speaks in his 1908 *Memoir* are, strictly

sion as known by the geometer sustains our point that an other space is not inconceivable.

iv. Space and Time not prior, but derived from events.

In the mathematical background of the theory of Relativity we find suggestion for a concreter conception of spatial plurality, without resorting to a radical subjectivism like that of Leibniz. It is found in the judgment that space and time are neither prior entities nor forms conditioning experience, but are *derivative from events*.

If space and time are, as Kant thought, necessary preconditions of experience, we could imagine their "contents" to vanish, but could not conceive the vanishing of these forms. If, however, they are derivative from events, then if events vanish we have left—not empty space-time —but exactly nothing. The arrival of an event brings with it its own *possibilities of relatedness*, spatial and temporal; and any such arrival constitutes a reckoning zero, a "middle" of all space and time, as thoroughgoing relativity requires, and experience tends to confirm. And as a corollary—the point that concerns us—*events independent of one another would have independent spaces*. Since space is not a prior reality into which any event must arrive and find orderly place, the genesis of events is governed by the nature of reality, not by the nature of space. If two events, or sets of events, were independent in origin, the space relations emanating, so to speak, from their centers could be infinite and plural, not alone without clash, but without any possibility of intersection, or even of tangency. This conjecture, at present abstract, will come to life as we proceed.

---

speaking, plural estimates of spatial intervals, in which space and time are so far interrelated that the quantitative estimate of each is a function of the other. Coexisting plurality had not become a conscious problem.

v. Problem: To define "the whole of space."

For our present space, this whole might be expressed as the totality of positions related to a given position by direction and distance. From every point in space to every other there is an imaginary line of determinate length; hence in the expression stated, no point would be omitted.

A more graphic way of putting it is to consider the path of an expanding sphere, with any given point, p, as a center, and increasing its radius, r, continuously from zero, without limit. The surface of such a sphere would obviously sweep all positions in the given space.

To express this conception in simple mathematical terms, consider "the whole of space" made up, not of points, but of volumes. At any stage of the sphere's expansion, the sphere has a surface of $4\pi r^2$. Now with a minimal expansion, lengthening the radius by a vanishing increment, dr, the advancing surface covers a thin shell whose volume is $4\pi r^2 \cdot dr$. And by adding such shells without limit—and of course timelessly—we traverse all of space, as expressed by the integral of all such shells:

$$4\pi \int_{r=0}^{r=\infty} r^2 \cdot dr$$

The arbitrary element in this expression is the choice of a center, as implied in the phrase "any point." Suppose we adopt some other point, p', however distant, and start another sphere with radius r' on the path of expansion. The two spheres will eventually interpenetrate, each including every position swept by the other. In other words, the two expressions are, not equal, but identical:

$$4\pi \int_{r=0}^{r=\infty} r^2 \cdot dr \quad \equiv \quad 4\pi \int_{r'=0}^{r'=\infty} r'^2 \cdot dr'$$

This identity merely formalizes the observation of Kant that all "spaces" are parts of the same space; from which he drew the inference that space could have no plural. But *this same identity* enables us to state with precision the condition under which there may be *more than one space*.

vi. Problem: Given a total space, to define the condition for "another space."

Since every point in a given space is related to every other point by distance and direction, then if there were a point *not so related* to a given point, it would be not in the given space, but would identify an other space. Express the interval between p and p' by the expression $p' - p$. If $p' - p$ exists, the total spaces about these two points are identical. Then the criterion for a point *not* in the given space is simply:

The interval, $p' - p$, *does not exist*.

Does experience present any such situation?

Quite frequently, in fact; though our path of recognition can most simply be taken by way of spaces intended or imagined. I dream of being in a canoe on a stream, waterfall ahead; just before the plunge, I waken: what is the distance between the prow of my canoe and the bedpost? $p' - p$ does not exist. A mathematician plots the loci of two curves in hyperbolic space, intersecting let us say in the point p': what is the distance between that point p', not as penciled but as meant, and a point p on the drawing board? $p' - p$ does not exist. You hang on your wall a Chinese painting in which a mountain peak rises out of misty clouds: what is the distance between that peak and the floor of your room? To say that the question is nonsense—which is quite true—is but another way of saying that $p' - p$ does not exist.

In general, any point in actual nature and any point in a nature which I imagine, dream, discover in works of art, or contemplate in thought, will display this independence. The comment that these imagined spaces are also nonexistent will become relevant as our analysis proceeds; the present effort is simply to see what "another space" could mean, and for this purpose the imagined space offers the readiest and wholly valid illustration. The events there occurring are independent of actual events; their time is their own; they may "hold still"; we may revert to them as often as we please: it is not the space alone that is other—it is the entire world of events thus entertained in thought that is "another world." Its space-time order is endless, forward and backward: and that its infinitudes never coalesce with those of the factual space-time, never interfere, is the condition that gives our imagination, fanciful or purposive, its requisite freedom and scope. The enjoyment of drama depends on a projected independence of this sort, borrowing a portion of actual space for the action, which the beholder constantly notes—often to his vast relief—"does not really happen"!

vii. The transition between plural spaces.

In the cases mentioned, the transition is obviously *mental*. It consists in a shift of attention, in general under the control of the self. The matter of importance here is the natural ease of this transition. Absorbed in the story, we bury ourselves in its crisis: we are here and not here; we can emerge, we can return at will. This capacity, well considered, has much to say of the nature of the mind itself: it is definitely *not "within"* either of the spaces it thus spans; it is something different from, as actively "objectifying," each of the space worlds for which it holds so effortlessly the avenue of transition.

And since, when we deliberately attend to another space we do not lose awareness of the space of actuality, but keep both more or less "in mind," this mental channel is not alone a way of passage from space to space but also a way of linkage—may we say a *vinculum*—holding plural spaces within a brace of simultaneous awareness, though not of equal awareness. [3]

viii. The freedom of concrete choice entails plural spaces.

In deliberating between alternative courses of action, I seek to "realize" what each course would involve: I use imagination with whatever responsible realism I can muster. The world I thus set before me is *intended to become* this actual world; but as contemplated it is other—as containing a nonexistent action, it may as a whole never reach existence. Prior to my decision, it has no power to exist; nor has the actual world any intrinsic power to contain what I now contemplate in idea.

Yet each such contemplated world is *possible*; the condition of its becoming actual is simply my decision. In regard to these possibilities, it is the self that determines nature, not nature that determines the self. The acting self is thus a *continual weaving of other worlds*, self-be-

[3] An architect working over his drawing may be sufficiently absorbed to forget any other space than that of his proposed building. Yet as the lunch hour approaches, it rarely occurs to him to resort to the cafeteria he has just included in the elevation. I agree that intensity of feeling and fancy may at times wear down the relative proportions of this fortunate duplicity.

gotten in thought, *into the texture of the present and given world*. The freedom thus exhibited is concrete, in the sense that it *alters the particulars* of the event sequence of the actual time-space manifold.

Current theories of freedom-of-will generally lack this element of concreteness, even though freed from the vision of physical monism which bound Kant and nineteenth-century thought. Looking at human action as a phenomenon of behavior in an objective world, the physical context of bodily motion still demands scientific loyalty; and the mental aspect of decision can for the behaviorist only be regarded as a subjective point of view of what in terms of actual history has its natural determinants. Royce's suggestion that natural process has, in certain situations, an open future in its ongoing, like an equation with multiple roots, has pertinence; but is necessarily limited to rare conditions of equilibrium. The same must be said, I think, of Arthur Compton's use of the ambiguities of prediction in nuclear physics. Whitehead's theory that the physical opportunity for freedom is to be found in the moment of noninteraction between events strictly simultaneous is even more limited in its scope. The freedom that concerns us is a *difference-making freedom* in the realm of overt action; and our philosophy is out of joint with experience until we do justice to this item of certitude in our human intuition of *power-to-create* in the world process.

This step, our prior analysis of our judgments of space and spaces, now enables us to take.

ix. If we now ask *how concrete freedom is possible*, in view of the firm nexus of causality in nature systems within which our bodies are engaged, the answer is at hand.

While the self as hinge of transition between worlds, a world of possibility and a world of actuality, is (by vii) not a member of either world, the body through which it acts is a member of each world thus contemplated. This implies that the body is in some degree numerically different in different worlds, as involved in the differing contemplated actions. For example, as one contemplates joining a skating party, the body as skating is numerically different from the body at rest while contemplating. The body of the dreamer seldom intrudes itself in dreams, yet when it does, it often illustrates Schopenhauer's concept of physical form as expressing the mode of life chosen by the "will to live." (For example: as a bird's wing expresses a will to live by aid of flying, so if one has the somewhat frequent dream of flying or of moving through the air, his bodily equipment accommodates itself to the function, without asking precise physiological sanction!) In every case, the body remains (as Aristotle rightly insisted) unique to the individual person: as against Pythagorean or Platonic transmigration, the soul of Peter cannot appear in the body of Paul. Yet Aristotle was wrong (as we have pointed out [4]) in inferring that an individual person could have but one body, uniquely expressing his quality and behavior: the very identity of the person would entail, in divergent situations, divergent physical expression.

In sum, the body—which expresses and identifies the acting person—is a function of two independent variables not of one only: it is in part, with life itself, a gift of "fact," but also in part a function of the self, serving that self's decisions and its capacity to create what, apart from the self's thought, the *world would not contain.*

And when we consider that human life, in its most gen-

[4] Pp. 32–34 above.

eral aspect, can be described as the continuous free translation of dream into fact, by way of bodily action, we
see how *the plurality of spaces makes concrete freedom
possible.*

In conceiving the shape of the deed to come, there is a
mutual creation: the man makes the idea, and the idea
makes the man. He is receptive—it "occurs to me"—
"es fällt mir ein"—and yet it *did not pre-exist*: it completely misrepresents the event to consider (with Whitehead) the arriving idea as an ingression or a prehension
or selection from a fixed "realm of eternal entities," in
which case no genuine novelty could occur. Creativity is
a genesis of possibilities of quality which, prior to the
begetting deed, had not even a positional existence: there
is *no such totality* as "all the values" nor "all the ideas,"
still less, "all the solutions." The thinker's mind, bent on
his inarticulate goal, as if in prayer, encounters blank
nescience; and then one day comes a swift light, unpre-
dictably transforming both the vista and the viewer; not
as a gift from prearranged discernments, but through
some intimate co-operation of thinker and object, comes
the viable idea striving for birth: "Now I see!" Tschai-
kowski laboring in despair over his keyboard resolves to
continue making sounds, no matter what, until the musical
ideas come: one day they begin to arrive, and then more
and more, beyond his capacity to record them. One day,
again, he pens the second movement of his sixth symphony, and we are tempted to say, not the possible but the
impossible—at any rate the nonpossible—has become a
possession of mankind.

The idea, once conceived, must be free to live its pre-
natal life, in the uncommitted space-time of deliberation,
until launched by decision into the space-time of the ac-

BD Hocking, William Ernest
4/21
H62
1973

The meaning of immortality
in human experience

③

tual. The self, as agent of transition, gives birth: there is creation in the world of fact. This is concrete freedom.[5]

x. The conditions for the possibility of concrete freedom are at the same time conditions for the possibility of survival.

I do not say sufficient conditions, nor yet necessary conditions: I say simply that insight into the possibility of concrete freedom opens an avenue of insight into the possibility of survival.

Whoever is concretely free is co-creator in an actual world: as such he is not *in toto* passive to the internal processes of that world. In the devising of free deeds within the context of particular fact, there is a literal sense in which *the self is in presence of at least one other space world all the time.* And to recognize this self as the vinculum, or hinge of transition, between these two space worlds, and as such not a member item in either of them, separates the destiny of that self from the total operation of causes playing within the world of nature.

To put the matter somewhat technically, our situation is as follows: the scientific picture of physical monism continues—throughout all revolutions of cosmology—to consider nature as a "closed group" of events, such that

[5] Professor Dobzhansky's current book on *The Biological Basis of Human Freedom* (Columbia Press, 1956) rightly recognizes that "the ability of man to choose freely between ideas and acts . . . perhaps . . . the most important of all the specifically human attributes" is something different in principle from the "necessity comprehended" of naturalism, whether of Marx, Spinoza, or Einstein: it is not deducible from biological laws (p. 134). Ethics, as one manifestation of freedom, "have no genetic basis and are not the product of biological evolution" (p. 132). Fairly summarizing the results of biological and genetic inquiries on this point, the book thus candidly indicates both the place and the need for a metaphysical analysis such as is here offered.

combining of events within the system of physical nature yields other events within the same system, never anything else. If there were a plurality of such closed systems, the *relation between them* could never be expressed in terms of the internal processes of any of them. But the mind is essentially such a relating entity or vinculum, holding before itself, in contemplating action, a plurality of such closed groups, as if it were itself a most general field in which space-time fields could coexist, a "field of fields" so to speak.[5] Hence the existence of the mind can be *no function of events within any of its object systems.*

This being the case, the event of death, involving the body of the self belonging to some one nature system, does not necessarily involve the death of the self (nor of its body) as already envisaging other worlds, independent of the given world. Death may thus be relative, not absolute. And the transition in death, a mental transition, devoid of distance.

[6] The phrase "field of fields" as defining the relation of the mind to plural nature systems is open to technical question on the ground that the notion of a field, in physics or mathematics, implies an infinite manifold of elements constituting a continuous order. This condition is realized in the case of conceptual geometries, where the curvature of space is in question: the geometer does indeed conceive of a continuous manifold of possibilities here: his mind, in this respect, functions precisely as a field of fields. But it is not necessary to press the point: this phrase may be taken as a metaphor—it is the word form under which the resolving insight first appeared to me. The title of the paper, "Theses Establishing an Idealistic Metaphysics by a New Route," is one I should not now choose, since the term "idealism" has become in polemic highly ambiguous—not to be used without definition. The element of metaphysical idealism indicated by this outlook is not that what we call the actual world is created by *my* thought of it, but that since it is the nature of the self, in contemplating a free act, to evoke an other world in creative thought, destined to actuality, we have here the index of creativity in general: mind can beget world as world cannot beget mind.

xi. Other-world as imagined and as actual.

In illustrating the meaning of other-spaces and other-worlds, we have referred not to actual but to imagined or dreamed or contemplated situations (§ vi). The reason is evident: we can illustrate only with what everyone can verify in his own experience, namely, the other-worlds that universally coexist with the world of our common experience we call "actual." The only procedure open to us was that of taking the imagined (or projected) as evidence of the conceivable, and the conceivable as clue to the possible, on the postulate that the relation of the self to imagined or projected other-worlds is structurally identical with its relation to any possible other-world.

Obviously, we are not concerned with possible other-worlds closed to mind, if such a conception has any meaning: we are concerned only with other-worlds of possible *experience*, worlds to this extent subjective. The distinction that now concerns us is that between a world *merely* subjective, and one which is also actual or real. What does this distinction mean?

For the most part, the distinction is clear enough: we seldom confuse an imagined situation with an actuality, or an actuality with an imagination. As for dreaming, we commonly take the dreamed experience for actual while it is taking place (though it is possible to know that one is dreaming, and even to some extent to control the dream); but it is seldom that the act of waking fails to put the dream immediately into the class "subjective only." What are our waking criteria of the dream as subjective-only?

Dreaming is typically indistinct, shifting, incoherent, lacking consecutiveness either in the purpose of the dreamer or in the procession of events, hazy in its setting in memory and outlook. But all these marks are variable: dreaming does at times become vivid, consecutive, and fit for some narrative of adventure—worth telling at the breakfast table! It then approaches the character of actuality. Could we carry this approximation to the limit— let us say a perfect dream—would it then *become actual?* Or would there still be a distinction? Or, to put the question conversely, could the actual world of experience be justly considered a perfect dream, logically consistent in every linkage as dreams are not, but yet a dream from which one could waken and recognize its relative unreality? If not, what would be the discriminating character of the "actual"?

There have been numerous attempts to answer this question.

It has been proposed that the dream lacks *resistance.* The actual is obdurate, has its own "nature" or inner logic and pursues it indifferent to our wishes; whereas dream yields to flitting fancy and may be described (in terms of one strand of psychoanalysis) as "uninhibited fulfillment of repressed wishes." I can only say that this view shows extremely poor observation: dreamed objects and animals, like their actual counterparts, follow their own ways—not ours. The ancient Hindus knew far better. In one of the later Upanishads, when Prajapati, testing Indra, tells him that "He who moves about, happy in dreams, he is the Self; this is the Immortal, the Fearless; this is Brahman," [7] Indra, at first persuaded, returns dissatisfied. He reports that dream also "has its struggle, its pain, and its tears." If my own experience is at all

[7] Khandogya Upanished, VIII, 10. In Max Müller's translation, *Sacred Books of the East* I, pp. 138 f.

typical, dream is far more likely to present puzzle, danger, frustration, than fulfillment. Lack of resistance is certainly not the answer.

A more pertinent proposal is that the actual experience is *shared with others*; it is that to which we can call witnesses, whereas dreaming is usually a private episode. It is, in fact, all but self-evident that whatever can be a common experience with other selves cannot be merely subjective. Astrophysicist Arthur Eddington, like Tycho Brahe before him, was satisfied with this criterion. If I fear I am suffering an illusion, I call on you to look: "Do you too see what I seem to see?"—if so I am in my senses, and what I seem to see is *there*! As Eddington put the matter, the actual world is "external"—not merely to the body but to the mind of each individual; and "the motive for the conception of an external world lies in the existence of other conscious beings." [8] Their co-witness guarantees the actuality of the perceived vista. Are we satisfied with this criterion?

It is certainly a convenient and usually available test: as a rule, whatever is shared with others is actual. But might we not *dream those others*? If other selves must be our guarantee of valid physical experience, what is the guarantee of valid other selfhood? Until the present century there has been no rigorous answer to this question: solipsism—self-enclosed experience, including the pantomime of human companionship—has remained for many careful analysts a consistent, perhaps a necessary, hypothesis.[9] But analysis aside, for common experience is it

[8] Article, The Domain of Physical Science, in *Science, Religion, and Reality,* ed. Joseph Needham, p. 192.

[9] The most striking illustration of this quandary in the entire history of philosophy is the doctrine of Leibniz that the world is a system of monads. None of the monads has any genuine companionship, yet each

possible that there is something *self-validating* in the presence and conversation of a companion, so that I am unable to doubt his reality even while I am doubting sun, moon, and stars? Almost I answer Yes: as for the impression of reality, there is something more immediately convincing in the voice and face of a friend than in all the furniture of earth and heaven. I know this to be the case: I have sat by the side of a dying person and have seen a flash of recognition come into the eyes when all the rest was a blur of emptiness—a potent and terrible moment in which all certitudes fail but one. But we must push our skepticism to the limit: is confirmation by co-witnesses a sufficient and final test of the actual?

xii. Co-witness is not a sufficient criterion of the actual.

After all, co-witness, while offering circumstantial evidence of the actuality of things, and helping to confirm our private impressions, does not *constitute* that actuality. The world is itself, not because you and I agree that it is such: we agree in our findings because the world is itself, identical for all finders. Being is first, witness is afterward. In so far as experience is, as we say, empirical, all co-witnesses are obedient to a common *datum*—not making what is there, but receiving it. We have various *signs* of the actual, but what we require to know is what constitutes that self-identity.

We shall be helped at this point, if we make a distinc-

---

one, finding all the others mirrored in its private world panorama, has every experience of conversation, and with it the co-witness of the mirrored world of nature and event. The monad, in its conception, is thus a perfect definition of a perfect dream, indistinguishable from actuality—and yet purely subjective! In theory, it completely refutes the test of co-witness, until we penetrate the logic of solipsism. On this point, my book *The Coming World Civilization,* pp. 33–41, has some comment.

tion in our terms. Let "the actual" stand for what appears or occurs, the *phenomenon*, whatever is actually "there" for all observers. Let us reserve the term "the real," for the *source of the actual*, the originating activity of which our empirical attitude is the obedient receiver. Then our question becomes whether "the real" can ever identify itself in our experience, except as "the actual." Eddington thinks not:

> Many philosophers [he writes] seem to consider that the statement that the external world is real, adds some property to it not comprised in the statement that it is the part of our experience held in common; but I am not aware that anyone has made a suggestion as to what this property could be.[10]

We have a suggestion: the property in question is, in a word, *initiative*.

That receptivity which marks our empirical attitude toward the external world, the receptivity of *all* empirical observers toward what they "hold in common," implies an identical *activity* having an "outer" source. It is this activity, this outer initiative, whose identity accounts for the agreement of the witnesses; it is this—and not the agreement—which constitutes the reality of the experience. The whole sense of empiricism rejects the notion of a real whose nature is an inert lump of space occupancy: it is, or has, an activity which, as it affects conscious beings, reveals itself. Eddington is not far from this view when he doubts "whether you or I have the faintest notion of how the process of 'existing' is performed"; [11] for if there is a "process" of existing, its working will presumably *show through* as the "giving" of phenomena to which our "receiving" is the counter-act.

[10] *Op. cit.*, p. 196.
[11] *Ibid.*, p. 191.

And if our receptivity is at the same time an awareness of being given-to—and how can they be separated—the real as active giver must be within our awareness. To be aware of our dependence on an outer initiative for the grist of our experience is *to be aware of that on which we depend*: no awareness of relation without awareness of the relata. Hence what we call "the real," and not unjustly consider the object of endless search, the goal of metaphysics, is at the same time however obscurely *ever present to consciousness*—a fact of the utmost importance. In every act we deal with it; when we push we drive against it; when we judge things and events we are also at the same time judging *it*. And when we err in judgment, it is the real which persistently sets us right. So looking at experience, our conscious life appears as *a consecutive conversation* with the real. And if we ask, what then is "the real" in itself, the answer is that its being—whatever else it may contain—must include this conversation and all such conversations—it cannot be inanimate Fact.

With this conception of the Real, a universe of plural worlds would effectively retain its core of unity, and at the same time provide the criterion for distinguishing our actual worlds from the merely subjective. The oneness of an identical Thou constitutes the vinculum among worlds that appear as "actual" to receiving subjects; awareness of this givenness constitutes the "realist" element in experience; the merely subjective worlds represent the "idealist" creativity of the individual subjects. Whatever human experience continues its experimental conversation with that Identical Thou *is itself* "*real*," whether its space-time context is of this world or of some other-world. And whatever human experience lets fall that conversation takes on the quality of dream, however well based on existing physical continuities. From such dream-within-life one might conceivably awaken, and then recognize *the relativity of "being alive."*

Herewith we reach a final answer to our question as to the distinction between a real world and a merely subjective world. The co-witness of fellow observers, a good symptom, is nothing more; it can have no finality unless we can be sure of *their* reality. The final mark of reality lies in the active source of the empirical data, the *recognized identity of the continuing respondent in all experience,* the giver of the given, the Real.

*   *   *

It was Descartes, I believe, who first stated to himself in set terms our problem (and Eddington's) : How can we be certain that our everyday waking experience is not subjective?—in Descartes' chosen figure it could be the deception of a malicious demon; What is the internal evidence of its reality? For Descartes there is no overt evidence of reality, and no immediate assurance; we must trust "the veracity of God," a God whose existence is evidenced by reason. In my view, the assurance of reality *is immediate*; because the experience of an actual world is at the same time an experience of its active source, the self-authenticating Thou-art. There is no need to rely on a "veracity of God," when our experience is an experience of God-at-work!

xiii. The outer-initiative which marks reality has its physical symbol, but is not physical "causation."

For the self-in-the-world, the excursive self, it is easy

to consider its receptivity as a passivity toward the direct action of nature. Most current theories of perception, referring our sense-data to physiological stimuli, invite us to revert to physical monism. As an inviting fallacy, let us note its error.

Physical monism leaves it a mystery why or how mentality enters the cosmic picture, and thus makes sense perception an unexplained superfluity. Its very perfection of self-enclosure cancels its claim—not as a postulate of scientific method—but as a metaphysic, an account of the real.[12]

For, after all, what marks the real is not simple activity, but original activity, begetting. The closed group of physical nature, even though it comprises the whole cosmic process in infinite space-time, is in essence *just one action*, endlessly transmitting (and conserving) itself through serially chain-bound configurations. Each phase of this action is accounted for by the preceding phase, with the all-important reservation that *unless the action-as-a-whole is accounted for, nothing is accounted for.* And since this one action fills the whole of time, it cannot be accounted for by any previous action: its source must be contemporaneous with all time and coextensive with all space.

The generating real, therefore, *cannot be a "cause,"* for a cause is always prior. A presumed "first cause" as uncaused could have no place in the time series; and

[12] Its case is not saved by the growing evidence that the observer has to be included in the meaning of operational results, or that field theory alone—as Hermann Weyl has pointed out in view of the atomicity of quanta—is insufficient to describe the data. Physical definitions involving the operator, still give no physical function to the relation "consciousness of."

would therefore not be strictly speaking a cause. A time-less or eternal cause appears to be a contradiction in terms, especially if what is caused is a temporal sequence of events (though a certain analogy may be seen in the light beam which sustains continued action in a moving picture —a condition *sine qua non* of the whole event series, with-out being itself one of the events). But the generating real may be *a communication*—always contemporary. As merely conserving what is there, physical process has no assignable motivation; *telos* is excluded. If, on the other hand, there is a meaning in process, it must be *found in something distinct from its conservation, a factor of creativity* which, to become adequate to emerging novelty, must include creators in what is created.

xiv. The criterion of reality is creativity, both for the world and for the individual.

Creativity is an affirmative power, though its under-standing may best be achieved in terms of what it is not. It is not mere wandering into novelty, nor is it selection from a pre-existing magazine of ideal ends. It is a giving-birth from an eternal Meaning, undefined except in vague terms of Good, or Right, or Beauty, whose being is a yearning for exemplification in irrational fact: creativity gives personal specification to the undefined. It is the reverse of an impersonal principle: it is personality in action.

With this view of the real, human living becomes not alone a consecutive experiment in judging the world; it becomes a *school in achieving one's own reality*, through learning to create—to conceive what deserves realization, and to realize some part of that conception. As an I-think, the self does indeed *exist*—Descartes is, so far, valid; but it remains *less than real* unless it becomes also a *source of being*, a partner in a total world-task of creation.

Herewith we dismiss, as Kant does, the Cartesian argument for immortality. It remains true that it is only the I-think, the person-as-subject, that can become creative, and therefore in any degree real. And from our own meditation we conclude that one's capacity, or call, to survive the physical crisis of death is no foredoomed necessity, but dependent on the measure in which one's use of freedom has charged the merely-existing I-think with genetic power.

This does not mean a solitary power to endure, as if an individual I-think could evolve into an indestructible monad. For "power" of any sort is power-in-a-context. The value-begetting power we speak of can only be a power to continue the participation in world-making with the identical Thou-art that has been its former life. If *per contra* there could be a totally unloving soul, using creative force for its own dream, as a monad, its solitude would be its non-existence for the living world: its perfect monadism would be its eternal death.

Herewith philosophical analysis must rest its case. Without broaching theological issues, it notes the possibility of a *self-executing justice* in the world-process, whereby what we refer to as the Will of God appears to each soul as the necessary outcome of its own willing: no soul shall perish but by its own consent. In its major description, the continuance of world-process *is* the fertile continuance of personal lives.

THE REACH OF EXPERIENCE

ANALYSIS is not solution: it offers truth, but something short of *the* truth. Its function is, not to replace intuitive persuasions regarding life and death, but to cure the vagrancy of a feeling-driven imagination, ready to substitute itself for truth. The deeper the hold of feeling on any issue, the sterner must be the resolve that feeling be disciplined by analysis, and not only for the sake of truth, but for the sake of feeling. For feeling has its own truth and falsity; and the *truthfulness of feeling*, quite as much as of thought, is an issue of life and death which a self-indulgent civilization has not yet begun to fathom. Without truth, feeling is corrupt: but conversely, without feeling, truth is barren. A true analysis must still seek its full truth in its organic unity with feeling.

Our analysis has turned on certain familiar concepts—the self, physical nature, freedom, reality, creativity. The term "creativity" became for us a token of reality, on the ground that that which only conserves cannot so much as explain its own presence in the universe. But "creativity" as a descriptive concept presents a trap, as a fallacious attempt to naturalize a primitive wildness and give it the decor of scientific standing. Let us be clear that

245

as an impersonal principle of world-process creativity falls lifeless: there is *no creativity in the universe without feeling*—or more specifically, without a subjective factor, an inner urge, whose nature is akin to what we call "love."

If this is the case, human destiny turns on the nature and potency of love; and love, in its most general sense, as the life of our own creativity—that is to say, of ourselves—needs less to be defined than to be recognized in self-consciousness, in immediate experience. We have only to confirm, as primary authorities, what Plato or the depth-psychologists, as secondary authorities, may tell us: that there is a *total élan* of our being toward an undefined goal, that the various impulses welling up in us through the subconscious tend to merge in a single self-sublimating Eros. And this central and pervasive longing presents to us images of total fulfillment, as it has to the race through all reflective history.

There are two great symbols of such fulfillment, that of the Beatific Vision of "The Good," and that of Creating through vesting our total *élan* in specific objects, the love of things, beings, persons. The beatific vision, putting an end to striving, dissolves time itself as individual experience. Creating-through-love is within the time-field and portends continued creation in time. Broadly speaking, the classic Orient (together with the neo-Platonic strain) tends to find fulfillment in the time-transcending vision; the West, in the continued working of love through time.

Our further understanding of human survival will depend on referring this issue to experience—experience of two kinds, first that of love itself, and then that of death. We shall briefly carry out this self-consulting inquiry: we shall find, I believe, that *Immortality involves both* modes of fulfillment.

1. THE EXPERIENCE OF CREATIVE LOVE

Love, as we commonly mean it, is specific: it is of things, beings, persons. Its horizon is indeed beyond them, it is *toward* something universal discerned in and through these particulars—the undefined object of our *total élan*. Love as a passion tends to vest its total fulfillment in individual objects, as the theme of its most tangible creativity.

The first impulse of specific love—and I include in love the response of the mind to beauty—appears less like a will to create than like a will to hold, to detain, as a step toward possession: *Verweile doch, du bist so schön*. But even this primitive impulse is the reverse of a state of repose: it is a haunting drive to know that being through and through, to grasp in thought the secret of its being, to obliterate its otherness and merge with it. Not literally to possess—though that term is used—for the free being is not to be destroyed in its freedom; but to be possessed in thought, and so to be reproduced, for we fully conceive *only what we make*. (This is the primitive motive of honest art—not imitation, not invention, but an ever-continuing appropriation of the real through one's own begetting.)

And thus to love is to treat the loved being as worthy of permanence. The impulse of caring is to hold that being forever above the accidents of time and death—as if one could! The miracle of love is that it so spontaneously forgets its own limitations: it assumes its right to act *in loco Dei*—and with the right assumes also its capacity! The pathetic folly of human affection? Or is it the reverse, a point at which human finitude rises to the point of participating in deity? I propose that here, in willing to confer immortality on another mortal, the self is in that moment reaching a deeper self-consciousness, an intimation of its own destiny.

Even so, the will to immortalize is not the whole of what we mean by the creative power of love. Nor is it limited to biological begetting. Human loves in their biological symbols of overcoming death achieve only the transfer of mortality, a possibly endless series of ending lives. Creative love does not leave the loved being unchanged: here the remoter horizon of the total *élan* or eros is to be remembered. It is this universal's fulfillment that is to be realized in the particular: in the savage-prophetic words of Nietzsche, "All great love is the beloved to create; and all creators *are hard*." What is loved, whether in persons or in nature, is never static perfection: in persons it is "the pilgrim soul," led on by that same vision—an unrealized self, striving toward what it *is* not, but has potency for. The life of the lover—aware not alone of what is, but of what is unborn possibility in the beloved—is in bringing that possibility to birth under the egis of the shared (though undefined) goal. Thus love becomes the energy of a continuous creativity in time.

And since the unrealized but germinal self has the dimension of infinitude, the *mission of love in time is never done*. Unless such love holds in itself an assurance of its own perpetuity, it moves under the shadow of a cosmic deceit.

We turn to inquire whether the experience of dying can throw any light on the field of this potential shadow.

2. THE EXPERIENCE OF DYING

We are not without ability to follow this experience for part of its course. There is the empathic observation, definitely perilous from the standpoint of truth, of the *witness* of dying; there is the report of persons who have gone *part way* into death and have returned; there is a broad stream of *tradition* from alleged seers, whose credentials we ourselves must judge.

As observers, we have to recognize the fact that when death is drawing its outline to a life, there is often on the part of the dying person an *apparent welcome* to terminus. Occasionally there is a more affirmative attitude, a certain "being in love with death" as if the dying were attracted toward nescience; such reversal of the will to live may invade life even before death approaches—as with Mozart, or Rilke, or O'Neill. There is such a thing as a normal will to die.

In the Orient, voluntary relinquishment of life has a respected place. A former student of mine, Dr. N. N. Sen Gupta, psychologist at Lucknow, gave me in 1931 an account of his uncle's predicted, and presumably controlled, death during a morning dhyana. Throughout Yoga-land one meets such accounts; Norman Hall relates some of them in his South Sea stories. Among us of the West, there is no such recognized art of purposefully stilling breath and heartbeat by direct will-control. But the foreknowledge and acceptance of the coming end, as by instinctive dismissal of *élan vital*, is not unknown. A friend tells of the farewell-to-life of her father's father:

As a very old man, he was accustomed to ask one of the children to stay home from work, to be with him, on days when he felt he needed care. One day he said a good-bye to each child, in a little ceremonious way which he had. Next day, on being asked whom he would like to have stay with him, he answered, "Nobody: I want to be alone today." In the evening, we found him as if asleep in his chair, dead.

In our world-region, for most of us, young or old, death

arrives in the midst of concerted efforts to fend it off, efforts accepted as obligatory and unquestioned. Yet, in my judgment, this is seldom the whole inwardness of the event for the dying. So far as I have been able to observe the approach of death, or to follow the observations of others, it has seemed possible to detect on the part of the dying person, in the later stages, a complicity with nature, as if, before dying were finished one became a consenting party. The following account appears to be fairly typical of death from disease:

> The patient was dying of TB. He had been unconscious, had reverted to a period of clear awareness, and had sunk back into coma. The physician said, "This is the last time; he will not come back." The nurse said, "Yes: he will come back." He came back twice—the second time only a moment or two before his breathing stopped. X was with him then, and he knew. Then without struggle he dropped away, as if in a deep welcoming of peace. When breathing and heartbeat stopped, the face composed itself into a beauty not to be described.

Such dismissal, if not reversal, of the will-to-live is independent of any judgment on the part of the dying that his work is finished: there are few who can say that. The dismissal supervenes on completed tasks, but also on broken-off labors—as with the King of Siam in the play, upon an "etcetera"—and on the deaths of the young. It seems to record a swift, infinitely relieving perception that *agenda are not the essence of living*; and that in some sense endings *should be* broken off. Otherwise one would regard his position in the universe as that of a spent Roman candle. Let the ever-seeking Faust but arrive at his goal, and—if it is the total goal—he has no future. The peace that comes to the dying is not that of terminus: it is—as I interpret it—the peace of *handing-on*, and of reverting to origins, with the felt opening of a perspective more profoundly valid.[1]

There are many reports of experience from persons who have returned from a part-way passage into death— and I have now in a minor way joined that company— reports which tend to confirm these conjectures. Gerald Heard will allow me to quote from a letter of May, 1951:

I believe the account given in Leo Tolstoy's remarkable short story, *The Death of Ivan Ilyitch,* is based on, and gives a vivid account not only of an actual experience, but of the experience which, in its main outline, will be ours when we "emerge"— when, as the Sanskrit text puts it, the grass core is drawn out from its sheath. That we do relinquish our restricted contact with the sensory world and pass into another frame of reference, I feel no doubt, both from my own experience and from those of others.

Drawing together these fragmentary data of experience, direct and indirect; and passing over a considerable body of literary evidence to the effect that death has a double aspect, that of enemy and that of friend;[2] we may interpret the experience of dying in its usual course somewhat as follows:

[1] But whether from a broken-off ending or from a sense of tentative conclusion, let me here record my conviction that though we of the West may have lost the power of relinquishing life by inner control, the normal will-to-die should be respected. With that will there also arrives the *right to die,* often cruelly denied or delayed, through a mistaken view of duty, abetted by the necessities of law.

[2] Much could be recorded of the widespread recognition in all cultures of the friendliness of death. Schubert's *Death and the Maiden,* with its terminal assurance, *"Bin Freund, und komme nicht zu strafen,"* may illustrate. And even in the more terrible forms of death, the note persists. A striking instance is found in the execution—some say the crucifixion—of the Persian mystic Al Hallaj in Baghdad, March, 922 A.D., done to death for blasphemy because he said "I am the Real." Al Hallaj had anticipated his fate, and had written:

After the earlier stages of detachment from identity with the body (in its socially expressive character), there occurs a sort of coming-forth into light, as in passing through a tunnel, an unshelling or emergence like the relief of a diver coming to the surface. The change which often comes over the features—an erasure of the marks of anxiety or suffering, a transfiguring into nobility and peace, a cosmic dignity—this visible change very probably registers a phase of the inwardly felt transition. Even before that point, we must distinguish between the experience of the dying person and the interpretations of the witness, based on normal expressive signs, except at moments of the dying person's return to recognition. There is ground to believe that the dying one tends early to separate his own being-in-the-world from that of his body, as if to say "Where art thou, pain?" And while the welcoming of death has in it a certain natural acquiescence in the growing weariness of a failing organism, a physically conditioned immense relief on "entering into rest"; this welcoming appears to be typically far more affirmative, as if new elements of experience and insight had entered consciousness.

Slayer, I hail thee with my dying breath,
Victor, I yield the fortress of my heart.
The doors fly open, and the poor lips part
Once more, and then no more, world without end.
The cup is poison, and the thought is death;
And He that gives them,
                    is not He the Friend?

This was his faith; it was also his deed. "During his execution," says Nicholson, "which was carried out in a barbarous manner, Hallaj displayed the utmost fortitude." (Hastings VI, 480–82.) He left upon his tormentors an undying impression of inner elevation.

3. THE BEATIFIC VISION AS FULFILLMENT

There is much in what we have noted to suggest that death brings a cessation of experience in time, whether as eternal absorption of the person in the One, as in the concept of Nirvana, or some other type of the beatific vision, consummatory and terminal.

The Hindu conception has its profound insights, based on its legitimate demand that religion and philosophy must found themselves on experience, a "direct awareness of the ground of existence." [3] The essence of this view is not in the notion of Karma—for Karma as the transmission of defective action through successive rebirths is not true immortality. "The real self, which is eternal and universal, does not undergo change." Its innate identity with the One cannot be discarded, though it is disguised and hidden under empirical conditions: its ultimate aim is to recover self-awareness. As Vivekananda inclined to put the matter, "Nature . . . takes the self-forgetting soul by the hand . . . bringing him higher and higher . . . till his lost glory comes back, and he remembers his own nature." The clamorous ego, insisting on its separateness from others and the One, is finally "cut away": after this consummation, no more experience-in-time.

There is no lack of spontaneous agreement with this outlook in western literature, so far as it, too, is based on direct experience, rather than on traditional imagery. Consider this plea of Siegfried Sassoon in *Sequences*:

[3] Swami Asashananda, "Hindu View of Immortality," in *Prabuddha Bharata*, February, 1957, 51 ff. The following quotations in this paragraph are from the same article, recording an address given at Northwest Philosophical Conference, U.S.A., 1956.

> I think
> If through some chink in me could shine
> But once—O, but one ray
> From that all-hallowing and eternal day,
> Asking no more of Heaven,
>   I would go hence.

In that summary "go hence," what powerful quitclaim of all lien upon the continuing universe! And yet without surrendering the claim of right, upon which I have insisted, as against the world that has produced us, the right to understand! Then willingly cease?

4. THE UNION OF VISION AND TIME

I recur to my suggestion that the two symbols of fulfillment *belong together*, and cannot truly be conceived in separation. As indicating how this is possible, let me point out that in fact the two modes of experience occur together in this life.

For the course of common living is not without its occasional "rays from that eternal day." Recall the experiences of "illumination" of which John Masefield speaks (*So Long to Learn*, 179 f.). They come—I believe to everyone in some degree—into our most desperate gropings: they offer—for an hour, a day, a group of days—a vision of the meaning of things: "Now, for the first time, I *see!*" Such in-lighting is not a termination: it is a new beginning. The glow vanishes, but the enlightenment remains, unbanishable. And the life-action that follows is lifted and directed by a unique sense of initiation—as if by a new hold on an *a priori* one should always have been living by—an awakening that knows its own awakeness— no completed truth, but an anticipation of ultimate attainment.[4]

[4] *The Meaning of God in Human Experience*, 30 f.

This, if I am not mistaken, is the true sense of the Hindu Jivanmukta, release within present existence. For the true eternity is time-inclusive, not time concluding. It spans the future, but *also the past*. Its insight often arrives (as does every valid *a priori*) with a sense of recollection, as if one were recurring to a past perception, long forgotten. The forward-looking longing transforms itself into a nostalgia. Plotinus has marvelously expressed this double time-reference of the impact of physical beauty:

> perceived at the first glance,
> It is evident that there is such a quality,
> recognized by the soul as something long familiar,
> arresting and beckoning. [Ennead I, vi, 2]

So if, in death, some fragment of the beatific vision should be our lot, arresting and beckoning the passing spirit— one who had already known love in its truthfulness—it would be indeed a glimpse of eternity, and a oneness with the One: but not a terminus of time in eternal changelessness. For the time which can be untimed, *at a time*, is not ended. It would be at once self-recovery, remembrance, and the continued lure to create through love in ongoing time. Our oneness with the One is participation, not in fixity, but in partnership with him that continually labors and creates, world without end . . .

INDEX

Montague, W. P., 170
Monuments, 8, 55, 85
Mystery, xvi, 54, 163, 170, 190 ff.
Mystic, 96, 156–63, 172
Mysticism, 127
Myth, 145, 162, 173 f., 176, 196, 197

Naturalism, xii, 24, 117, 170, 172 f.
Natural piety, 121
Nature, 26, 54, 64
as closed group, 233
Negative wholeness, 48, 52, 54, 66, 154
Newton, I., 221 f.
Nietzsche, F., 99, 248
Nirvana, 172, 253
Novelty, 99, 137, 179, 182, 243

Objectivity, 136, 153
test of, 238
Obligation (*see also* Duty), 120
of the universe, 7
One, The, 253, 255
Opportunity, 15
Organism, organic, xii, 24, 49
Orient, 124
its view of destiny, 196, 246
voluntary death, 249
Other, -ness, 26, 28, 65, 138, 220, 234
Other world, 25, 63
imagined and actual, 235 ff.
Otherworldliness (*see also* Detachment), 25, 125 f., 172

Paradise, 105
Paradox, -es of meaning, 98, 133, 157
Parapsychology, 21, 211–15
Participation, 247, 255
Particulars, 106, 134, 142, 160, 230
Peace, 250
Perception, 36, 242
Perfection, 6, 134, 146
Perishing, 179, 183, 188
Person, -ality, 187, 205, 244
Personalism, 199
Pessimism, 10, 99, 108

Philanthropy as immediate value, 95
Philosophy, responsibility of, 77, 105 f., 107, 156
Physicalism, 38, 121
Physical monism, *see* Monism
Physical world, as closed group, 183
Pilgrim soul, 92, 248
Plato, 30, 33, 34, 70, 71, 75, 91, 123, 134, 144, 197 f., 246
Play, 85
Pleasure, 111, 124
Plotinus, 255
Poet, poetry, 30
and truth, 175, 204
Positivism, 21
Possibility, 52, 62, 63, 154, 202, 210, 221, 229
Postulate, -s, 27, 191
Power, -s, 48, 158, 244
Pragmatism, 106, 113, 120, 123, 129, 150, 157
Pratt, J. B., 204
Pre-existence, 199 f.
Prehension, 184
Primitive, 107, 108, 168, 175
as significant, 176
Probability, 3, 22
Process, *see also* Flux, 244
Prophetic consciousness, 158
Proof, 3, 23, 67
Proust, 151
Psychiatry, psycho-analysis, 103, 118, 141, 169
Psychology, 33, 44, 53, 114, 116
Ptah Hotep, 124
Pythagoras, 200
Pugnacity, 17, 127

Question, -ing, 141 f.

Ratchet, 83
Real, -ity, x, 24, 40, 76, 135, 151, 239, 244
achievable in degree, 75, 147, 153 f.
ambiguous, 41